ABOUT THE AUTHORS

 Just Around the Curve is the fourth cookbook co-authored by Sharon and Gene McFall. Their first was the beautiful and informative *Cookin' with Will Rogers*. Next was the national best-seller, *Busy Woman's Cookbook*, followed by *Get Me Out of the Kitchen*.

SHARON MCFALL is a native of Des Moines, Iowa, and has worked extensively in publicity and promotion and in the retail management field.

GENE MCFALL is a former teacher and basketball coach from Kentucky. Since 1982 he has performed as an actor in his nationally acclaimed one-man show, "Witty World of Will Rogers", appearing in 45 states and around the world.

When Sharon is not collecting recipes and writing, she books and promotes Gene's show. This husband and wife team's mutual love of cooking has inspired them to write cookbooks. In their collaboration, Sharon researches and collects the recipes, works on the layout and design, and Gene researches and does the stories and other material, but they do sometimes overlap each other's duties—tactfully.

home of L,L, Bean. The 50 acre Deserts of Maine has drifting sands, windswept dunes up to 20 feet high, and camel statues. It was created by melting glaciers in the ice age. Over the centuries it was covered with soil, grass and trees. Timbering and over grazing in the 1800's allowed the wind and weather to expose it again.

Maine's 5,500 miles of coastline and 6,000 inland lakes and ponds have helped inspire artists from Winslow Homer to Andrew Wyeth. The Maine Art Museum Trail comprises seven museums with more than 53,000 works of art.

Just Aroun

he Curve

New Hampshire, was the first American state to declare indepen- dence. The state has no sales tax or personal income tax. An alternate source of revenue is state owned liquor stores which sell on Sundays, unlike their neighboring states.

Have you heard the term "filthy rich?" You will know what it means at the shore along Ocean Avenue in **Newport, Rhode Island**. Dozens of industrial barons at the turn of the 20th Century built their "summer cottages" here–huge, elaborate 60 room mansions. Among them are the home of Jackie Kennedy Onassis' family, the Breakers (the largest), and one of the most elaborate ($10 million in the 1890's), the Vanderbilt's Marble House.

ACKNOWLEDGEMENTS

 As we travel across the United States, and folks we meet find out that we write cookbooks, they are delighted to share a favorite recipe with us. They are often written on a napkin, a paper sack or a restaurant menu. We often receive them later by mail or fax. Small town restaurants are often happy to give us a recipe of which they are proud. We offer special thanks to all the wonderful people who have contributed their delicious recipes.

We have many friends who travel extensively in their motor homes. We asked them questions and sought their advice about what would make an interesting and useful cookbook for travelers. For their insight, helpfulness and encouragement we are especially grateful.

Thanks to our daughter, Linda Burgett, who spent many hours getting this book ready to send to the designer.

FOREWORD

 Many years ago extended travel was very primitive. You either stayed in a "motor court" or pitched a tent. Any cooking was done over an open campfire.

Today many "full timers" do not even own a house. They spend all their time in a modern RV, many of which are fancier and more expensive than an average house. Many others spend weeks or months in their motor home on extended vacations or "snow birding" in the winter. Some people still prefer to pitch a lightweight, easy to set up tent, especially in more remote scenic areas.

But whatever method is used for life on the road, everyone must eat. Quickly the fast food restaurants get rather old, and the better restaurants can get expensive (and require at least shoes and a shirt.) So cooking at your campground or in your RV becomes a pleasant necessity.

Grilling is a favorite method, but not the only alternative. RVs come equipped with ovens, ranges, microwave ovens and crockpots. But the traveling cook does not want long complicated recipes, nor do they want to have dozens of ingredients in a recipe. Ease and

The oldest European settlement in America is not **Plymouth, Massachusetts,** but is St. Augustine, Florida. It was founded in 1565 by European explorer Don Pedro Memendez de Aviles–55 years before the Pilgrims landed at Plymouth Rock.

Artist Norman Rockwell is probably best known for his covers for "The Saturday Evening Post" (322 of them). His studio was moved intact from behind his home in **Stockbridge, Massachusetts,** to the Norman Rockwell Museum overlooking the Housatonic River Valley. The museum has the largest collection of Rockwell work in the world, 570 pieces.

quickness of preparation are as equally important as delicious taste.

Just Around the Curve is specifically tailored for the needs of the rapidly growing traveling public. Crockpot recipes let you put it on in the morning, and when you stop that evening you have a tasty meal. Interesting grilling recipes keep you from having the same old hamburgers the same old way. Microwave recipes enable dishes to be fixed superfast. The recipes for range top or traditional ovens are chosen for their ease of preparation as well as for their culinary quality.

Just Around the Curve is not just a cookbook for those on the go, but it is a great collection of recipes that will be a delight to use at home. So forget about long grocery lists and hours spent cooking and enjoy the great dishes from this book.

Start Your Engines

Beverages

Appetizers

Henry Ford started the Ford Motor Company in 1903. In 1908 he introduced the Model T, "a car for the multitudes." It was easy to service and very affordable. In 1908 it sold for $850, $440 in 1915, and dropped to $275 in the 1920's. You could buy it in any color you wanted, as long as it was black.

The world's fastest automobiles do not run on the super speedways at Daytona, Florida, or Talladega, Alabama, nor at the Indianapolis 500. They run on the Bonneville Salt Flats in Utah. The ancient dried lake beds make a great flat surface for setting world land speed records–over 400 mph for a two-way, one-mile run.

In the late 1890's Charles Duryea won the first automobile race at the average speed of 5 miles per hour on a 50 mile race course around Chicago. He and his brother had built the first American motor car in Springfield, Massachusetts. By 1910 speeds had increased dramatically. Barney Oldfield set a record of over 131mph at Daytona Beach, Florida. The Indianapolis 500 race began in 1911.

Today the United States has over 175 million licensed drivers, over 200 million registered vehicles, traveling on more than four million miles of paved roads and highways.

AFTER A HIKE COCKTAIL

¼ cup sugar
1 cup cranberry juice
1 (6 ounce) can frozen orange juice
3 cups club soda, chilled

In a pitcher, combine sugar, cranberry juice, and orange juice. Stir until sugar dissolves. Cover and chill. Stir in club soda just before serving. Serve in a glass with ice. ◆Makes 5 cups.

A COFFEE PICKER UPPER

3 cups half-and-half
¾ cup maple syrup
3 cups strong coffee

In a medium saucepan, combine half-and-half and maple syrup. Heat over medium heat until hot (do not boil), stir in coffee. ◆Makes 6 cups.

HOT JUICE WARM-UPS

1 cup pineapple juice
1½ cups cranberry juice
1½ cups hot water
3 cups orange juice
1½ teaspoons lemon juice

In a 2 quart bowl, combine all ingredients. Microwave at high for 10 minutes. Serve in mugs. Garnished with thin orange slice. ◆Make 6 cups.

KANSAS TORNADO SHAKE

Cookin' with Will Rogers Cookbook

2½ cups cold milk
4 teaspoons instant coffee powder
½ cup chocolate syrup
1 quart chocolate ice cream

In blender container, add 1 cup cold milk, coffee, syrup, and ice cream, cover, blend until smooth. Add remaining milk and blend. Serve immediately. ◆Makes 6 servings.

START RIGHT HONEY SHAKE

2 oranges cut into bite size pieces
1 banana, sliced
½ cup low fat milk
1 teaspoon honey
¼ teaspoon vanilla
1 cup ice cubes

In a blender container, combine oranges, banana, milk, honey, and vanilla, cover and blend 30 seconds. Add ice cubes one at a time; blend 15 seconds after each addition. Pour into 3 tall glasses; sprinkle with nutmeg on top, if desired. ◆Makes 3 to 4 servings.

SHAKE AWAKE SMOOTHIE

1 cup cold brewed coffee
1 cup vanilla ice cream or vanilla frozen nonfat yogurt

In a blender container, combine all ingredients, cover. Blend on high until smooth. Serve immediately. ◆Makes 2 servings.

ANYTIME PEACH SHAKE

1 cup milk
1 cup sliced peaches
1 pint peach ice cream
1 tablespoon sugar

In a blender container, add ¼ cup milk and peaches, blend until smooth. Spoon in ice cream and blend until softened. Add ¾ cup milk and sugar, blend well. Pour into tall glasses. ◆Makes 4 servings.

TAILGATE PARTY PUNCH

1 quart bottle of cranberry juice cocktail, chilled
5 (12 ounce) cans orange soda
1 pint raspberry sherbet

In a large punch bowl, combine cranberry juice and soda. Scoop sherbet into mixture. Serve immediately. ◆Makes 9 servings.

One of America's most imaginative children's books authors was born in **Springfield, Massachusetts,** in 1904. The Dr. Seuss National Memorial Sculpture Garden there features cast bronze statues of his most famous characters-the Cat in the Hat, a 14 foot tall Horton the Elephant, the Big Hearted Moose, the Grinch and his dog, Max and other characters.

"Lizzie Bordon took an axe and gave her Father forty whacks. Then when she was done, she gave her mother forty-one." One of the most notorious murders in history took place in the small town of **Fall River, Massachusetts,** in 1892, and gave birth to the above verse. Lizzie was acquitted and lived out her life in Fall River. You can see the home where the murders (never solved) took place, Lizzie's later home and the cemetery where the participants in the drama are buried. Local residents still disagree as to Lizzie's guilt.

MAKING CONDENSED MILK

1 cup powdered milk
⅓ cup boiling water
⅔ cup sugar
3 tablespoons butter

In a blender container, combine all ingredients, cover and blend until sugar has dissolved and is smooth. If you do not use this right away, store it in the refrigerator. ◆Makes 2 cups.

SHOWING OFF FRUIT DIP

1 (8 ounce) package cream cheese, softened
1 (16 ounce) jar marshmallow cream
¼ cup diced strawberries
¼ cup diced grapes
¼ cup diced apples
¼ cup diced cantaloupe

In a large bowl, combine cream cheese and marshmallow cream, mix well. Blend in the fruit. Serve with fruit or veggies. ◆Makes 12 to 15 servings.

OH WOW! STRAWBERRY DIP

1 cup frozen strawberries

1 (4 ounce) package cream cheese, softened

¼ cup sour cream

1½ tablespoons sugar

In a blender container, blend strawberries until smooth. In a small bowl beat cream cheese until smooth. Stir in sour cream, strawberries, and sugar. Mix well, cover and refrigerate until ready to serve. Serve with assorted fruit. ◆Makes 6 servings.

A QUICK FRUIT DIP

1 (8 ounce) package cream cheese, softened

1 (16 ounce) carton cool whip

1 cup orange juice

In a blender container, combine all ingredients. Cover and blend until smooth. Chill before serving. Serve with assortment of fruit. ◆Makes 12 to 15 servings.

Although **Vermont** is noted for its fall foliage and maple syrup, the Shelburne Museum near Burlington has one of the greatest collections of Americana outside the Smithsonian. In more than 30 buildings (some restored) are housed art works, inventions and other memorabilia.

KICK BACK MEXI DIP

▼ *(Crock Pot)*

1 (16 ounce) can refried beans
1 cup shredded cheddar cheese
½ cup salsa
½ cup chopped green chili pepper

In a medium bowl, combine all ingredients. Place in a crock pot, heat 60 minutes or until cheese has melted. Serve with chips. ◆Makes 2 cups.

DYNAMITE DIP

Cookin' with Will Rogers

1 (16 ounce) carton sour cream
1 (1.5 ounce) envelope beefy onion soup mix
2 tablespoons chopped jalapeno

In a medium bowl, combine all ingredients, mix well. Serve with chips. ◆Makes 2 cups.

3 STEPS MAKE CHEESE DIP

▼ *(Crock Pot)*

1 pound Velveeta® Cheese
1 (10 ounce) can diced tomatoes and green chilies
1 teaspoon taco seasoning

Cube cheese and place in crock pot, cover and heat until cheese has melted, stirring occasionally. Stir in tomatoes, green chilies, and seasoning. Cover and cook on low for 60 minutes. Serve with tortilla chips. ◆Makes 6 to 8 servings.

YUMMY SPINACH DIP

1 (1.5 ounce) envelope dry onion soup mix

1 (16 ounce) carton sour cream

1 (10 ounce) package frozen chopped spinach, thawed and drained

In a large bowl, combine all ingredients, mix well. Chill. Serve with chips or fresh cut vegetables. ◆Makes 2⅓ cups.

CREAMY DIP FOR VEGGIES

½ cup sour cream

½ cup ranch dressing

½ cup Miracle Whip®

¼ cup grated Parmesan cheese

⅓ cup bacon bits

2½ tablespoons chopped green onion

In a large bowl, combine all ingredients, mix well. Refrigerate until chilled. Serve with cut up vegetables or crackers. ◆Makes 1½ cups.

Groton, Connecticut, is the hometown of the U.S. Naval Submarine Base, headquarters of the North Atlantic Fleet. The country's first nuclear-powered submarine, and the first to sail under the Polar Ice Cap, the USS Nautilus, was built in Groton in 1954. It is open for tours, as is the Submarine Force Museum next door.

The Barcelona Harbor Lighthouse on Lake Erie in **New York** was built in 1829. In 1831 it became the first lighthouse to be powered by natural gas. During Prohibition its beacon guided smugglers bringing booze from Canada.

SHORTCUT SHRIMP DIP

■*(Microwave)*

1 (8 ounce) package cream cheese

1 (10¾ ounce) can cheddar cheese soup

1 (4½ ounce) can shrimp

3 tablespoons diced green onion

Add cream cheese in a 1 quart casserole. Microwave for 1 minute at medium high. Add remaining ingredients and mix thoroughly. Microwave for 5 or 6 minutes at medium high just before serving. Serve warm with assorted crackers. For compact microwaves, use high instead of medium high. ◆Makes 8 to 12 servings.

LOUISIANA SHRIMP DIP

1 (8 ounce) package cream cheese, softened

1 (10¾ ounce) can cream of shrimp soup

½ teaspoon Louisiana style hot sauce

¼ cup diced celery

1½ tablespoons diced onion

In a medium bowl, combine all ingredients. Mix well and chill. Serve with crackers or chips. ◆Makes 2¼ cups.

LAST MINUTE CHOCOLATE DIP

1 cup sour cream

½ cup honey

½ cup unsweetened cocoa

1 teaspoon vanilla

In a medium bowl, combine all ingredients, mix well. Cover and refrigerate until ready to serve. Serve with assorted fruits. ◆Makes 1½ cups.

QUICK AS A WINK CHEESE BALL

1 (8 ounce) package cream cheese

1 (8 ounce) can crushed pineapple, drained

1 teaspoon seasoned salt

1 tablespoon diced onion

½ cup chopped nuts

In a medium bowl, combine all ingredients except nuts. Mix well. Roll mixture into a ball. Cover the ball in chopped nuts and chill. Serve with assorted crackers. ◆Makes 2 cups.

In 1905 it cost George Eastman (of Kodak camera fame) only $300,000 to build his 35,000 square feet home with 37 rooms, 13 baths, and 9 fireplaces. The colonial revival structure on a 12.5 acre estate in the heart of **Rochester, New York,** cost $1.7 million to restore in 1990.

You can get a beautiful view of Margate Beach and the Atlantic Ocean by looking through the eyes of Lucy, a six-story high, 120 year old elephant, at **Margate, New Jersey,** a suburb of Atlantic City. A 30 minute tour takes you up a spiral staircase in one of her hind legs to her stom-ach-painted Pepto Bismal pink.

ON A HOLIDAY CHEESE BALL

■*(Microwave)*

1 (8 ounce) package cream cheese
2 cups grated cheddar cheese
2 tablespoons diced onions
2 tablespoons apple juice
1/3 cup chopped pecans

In a 2 quart bowl, microwave cream cheese for 1 to 1½ minutes at medium high. Beat in cheddar cheese, onions, and apple juice until smooth. Chill slightly and form into a ball. Roll in pecans. Serve with assorted crackers. ◆Makes 12 to 15 servings.

MISSISSIPPI HAM BALL

1 (12 ounce) package sliced ham
1 (8 ounce) package cream cheese
3 green onions, chopped fine
1 teaspoon Accent seasoning

In a blender container, shred ham. In a medium bowl combine ¾ of ham, cream cheese, onions, and Accent sea-soning. Mix well. Roll into ball and coat with remaining ham. Serve with crackers. ◆Makes 6 to 8 servings.

CHEESE TUNA BALLS

Cookin' with Will Rogers Cookbook

2 (6 ounce) cans tuna, drained
1 (8 ounce) package cream cheese, softened
1 tablespoon lemon juice
2 tablespoons grated onion

In a large bowl, combine all ingredients except nuts. Form into ball and roll in nuts. Serve with crackers. ◆Makes 6 to 8 servings.

OKLAHOMA OKIE NUTS

¼ cup butter
2 cups walnuts
1½ tablespoons sugar
¼ teaspoon allspice
½ teaspoon cinnamon

In a medium saucepan, melt butter, add nuts. Stir gently over low heat for 2 minutes. Sprinkle nuts with sugar and spices mix until well coated. Pour on a cookie sheet until cool. ◆Makes 4 to 6 servings.

Philadelphia, Pennsylvania's Eastern State Penitentiary was the most expensive building in the U.S. when it was built in 1820 at the cost of $780,000. It stressed solitary confinement, designed to have 250 inmates in separate cells with private exercise areas. Its floor plan was copied in more than 300 prisons worldwide. It housed such criminals as Al Capone and bank robber Willie Sutton, who tried to tunnel out in 1945.

At Philadelphia's Independence Hall our nation came into being when the Declaration of Independence was framed by our founding fathers in 1776. Also in the building the Articles of Confederation were written as was the Constitution, the flag was adopted, and George Washington was made commander-in-chief of the Continental Army. Across the street is the Liberty Bell, whose inscription reads, "Proclaim Liberty throughout all the land unto all the inhabitants thereof."

NEW HAMPSHIRE SPICED NUTS

1 egg white
1 teaspoon water
1 cup pecans, slightly broken
1 cup salted peanuts
¾ cup sugar
1 tablespoon pumpkin spice

Preheat oven to 300 degrees. In a large bowl, beat egg white and water until foamy. Add nuts, sugar, and pumpkin spice. Spread on greased cookie sheet. Bake for 20 minutes. Cool on waxed paper. Break apart when cool.

PRETZEL TWIST NIBBLERS

1 (14 ounce) package pretzel nuggets
3 cups tiny twist shape pretzels
⅓ cup vegetable oil
1 (1 ounce) envelope ranch dressing mix

Preheat oven to 325 degrees. In ungreased 15½x10½ inch jellyroll pan, place pretzels. In a small bowl, combine oil and ranch dressing, mix well. Pour over pretzels. Bake for 10 minutes, stirring once. Cool. Store tightly covered. ◆Makes 8 cups.

CALIFORNIA FROSTY GRAPES

¾ cup sugar

2 (4 serving) box unflavored gelatin

10 small grape clusters

1 cup water

In a medium bowl, combine sugar and gelatin. Mix well. Dip grape clusters in water. Sprinkle sugar mixture over wet grapes. Place on waxed paper, let set 60 minutes. Arrange on serving plate. ◆Makes 10 servings.

PARTY PLEASERS CHICKEN WINGS

2½ pounds chicken wings, separated at joints, tips discarded

1 cup barbecue sauce

2 tablespoons maple syrup

1 teaspoon sugar

1 teaspoon Worcestershire sauce

Preheat over to 450 degrees. In 15x10x1 inch baking pan, lined with foil, place chicken. Bake for 30 minutes. Drain grease. In a small bowl, combine barbecue sauce, maple syrup, sugar, and Worcestershire sauce. Brush chicken wings with mixture. Bake an additional 15 minutes. ◆Make 6 to 8 servings.

Build your own pumpkin cannon, catapult or sling-shot and see how far you can "chunk" a pumpkin in Millsboro, **Delaware's** Pumpkin' Chunkin' Contest each November. The record is 4,114 feet.

HONEY AND SPICY BAKED WINGS

1 (1.5 ounce) envelope dry onion soup mix
½ cup honey
1 tablespoon spicy brown mustard
18 chicken wings, separated at joints, tips discarded

Preheat oven to 400 degrees. In a medium bowl, combine onion soup, honey, and mustard. Mix well. Brush chicken wings with mixture. In 15x10x1 inch baking pan, place chicken. Bake for 45 minutes, turning once. ◆Makes 30.

PARTY COCKTAIL WIENERS
▼ *(Crock Pot)*

1 pound package cocktail wieners
½ cup ketchup
½ cup barbecue sauce
½ cup brown sugar
⅛ teaspoon Worcestershire sauce

In crock pot, combine all ingredients, cover and heat on high one hour. Remove lid and cook on low an additional 50 minutes. ◆Makes 4 to 6 servings.

GRANDMA'S DEVILED EGGS

Busy Women's Cookbook

6 eggs, hard cooked
3½ tablespoons Miracle Whip®
⅛ teaspoon mustard
1 teaspoon sugar

Cut hard cooked eggs in halves, slip out yolks, in a small bowl, mash with fork. Mix in rest of ingredients. Sprinkle with paprika (optional). ◆Makes 6 to 8 servings.

NEW MEXICO RESTAURANT STYLE SALSA

Mild to Wild Mexican Cookbook

1 cup finely chopped fresh tomatoes
3 tablespoons finely chopped green
    onions
1 tablespoon finely chopped cilantro
1½ teaspoons lemon juice
2 teaspoons hot pepper sauce
1 teaspoon garlic powder
¼ teaspoon ground cumin
¼ teaspoon salt

In a blender container, combine all ingredients. Blend until it reaches the consistency you desire. Refrigerate at least one hour. ◆Makes 1¼ cups.

Near Sharpsburg in western **Maryland,** the Antietam National Battlefield was the site of the single bloodiest battle in the Civil War. In 1862 40,000 Confederates faced twice that many Union soldiers. In just a few hours 25,000 men lay dead or dying. The results were inconclusive, but it encouraged Lincoln to issue the Emancipation Proclamation. Aside from plaques and memorials the site is relatively unchanged.

GUACAMOLE SALSA

6 small ripe avocados, halved, pitted and peeled
¼ cup lemon juice
1 cup salsa
2 green onions, finely chopped
¼ teaspoon salt
¼ teaspoon garlic powder

In a medium bowl, mash avocados with lemon juice. Combine mixture with salsa, onions, salt, and garlic powder. Mix well. Serve with chips. ◆Makes 4 cups.

PEACHY SALSA

2 (8 ounce) packages cream cheese
1 (8 ounce) carton sour cream
1 (16 ounce) jar peach salsa

In a large bowl, soften cream cheese. Beat in sour cream. Add salsa. Mix well. Serve with tortilla chips. ◆Makes 6 to 8 servings.

ON THE SIDE
CRANBERRY RELISH

6 cups fresh cranberries

1½ cups sugar

1 cup water

2 tablespoons grated orange rind

In a large saucepan, combine all ingredients. Cook over low heat until berries burst. Cool. Can be refrigerated up to 8 weeks. ◆Makes 8½ cups.

CLUB HOUSE CHEESE SPREAD

1 (8 ounce) package cream cheese

½ cup cranberry orange sauce

3 tablespoons chopped pecans, toasted

Spread cream cheese on a serving plate. Top with sauce and sprinkle with pecans. Serve with crackers. ◆Makes 6 to 8 servings.

PIMENTO CHEESE SPREAD

1 (8 ounce) package cheddar cheese, grated

⅓ cup pimento stuffed green olives, sliced

¼ cup Miracle Whip®

In a medium pan, combine all ingredients, heat until smooth. Cover and chill. ◆Makes 2 cups.

You can test your psychic abilities on an ESP machine at the Association for Research and Enlightenment in **Virginia Beach, Virginia.** It was begun in 1931 to preserve and study the 14,350 "readings" of the clairvoyant, Edgar Cayce, 1877–1945, who diagnosed illnesses from a patient's letter. A Kentuckian, Cayce moved to Virginia because he felt it was an area of good psychic energy.

PUMPKIN BUTTER SPREAD

1 (15 ounce) can pumpkin
1 cup apple, peeled and grated
½ cup packed brown sugar
¾ teaspoon pumpkin pie spice
1 cup apple juice

In a medium saucepan, combine pumpkin, apples, brown sugar, spice, and apple juice. Bring to a boil; reduce heat to low, stirring occasionally. Simmer 1½ hours. Store in refrigerator for up to 2 months. ◆Makes 3 cups.

JUST A DELIGHT PINEAPPLE SPREAD

1 (8 ounce) package cream cheese, softened
1 (8 ounce) can crushed pineapple, drained
1 tablespoon mayonnaise

In a medium bowl, combine all ingredients. Beat until smooth. Spread on wheat or white bread. Cut each slice into 4 parts. ◆Makes 12 to 15 servings.

SUNNY AFTERNOON SLUSH

(Diabetic)

1½ cups buttermilk

⅓ cup orange juice concentrated, undiluted

2 tablespoons granulated sugar substitute

1 teaspoon vanilla extract

3 ice cubes

In blender, combine buttermilk, orange juice, sweetener, and vanilla. Cover and blend until mixed. Add ice cubes one at a time and blend. ◆Makes 4 servings.

Per Serving: *Exchange–⅔ skim milk, ½ fruit; Calories–87; Carbohydrates–17 g*

SMOOTH CHOCOLATE SIPPER

(Diabetic)

2 cups low fat ice cream

2 tablespoons chocolate flavoring

2 tablespoons mint flavoring

1 tablespoon chunky peanut butter

In a blender container, combine all ingredients, cover and blend until smooth. ◆Makes 4 servings.

Per servings: *Exchange–1 low fat milk; Calories–116; Carbohydrates–15 g*

The state of **Virginia** has produced eleven presidents, eight for the United States and three for Liberia. The Liberian presidents were free blacks from Virginia who served as president of the African nation during the early years of its independence-between 1848 and 1883.

The world's largest musical instrument may be the "Stalacpipe Organ" in Luray Caverns in **Virginia.** Three and a half acres of cavern are covered with stalactites which produce musical tones when tapped electronically with rubber tipped mallets. Leland Springle invented the "organ" in 1954.

CREAMY ORANGE FROST

(Low Fat/Low Calorie) Get me out of the Kitchen Cookbook

½ cup orange juice

½ cup mashed banana

1 tablespoon nonfat milk powder

⅛ teaspoon nutmeg

2 ice cubes

In a blender container, combine all ingredients, cover and blend until creamy. ◆Makes 2 cups.

Per serving: *Calories–68; Protein–1 g; Fat Trace; Carbohydrates– 16 g; Cholesterol–12mg; Sodium–12 mg*

CRANBERRY COOL DOWN COOLERS

(Diabetic)

2½ cups reduced calorie cranberry juice cocktail

1½ cups unsweetened orange juice

1¼ cups club soda, chilled

In a large pitcher, combine cranberry juice and orange juice, mix well. Cover and chill. Stir in club soda just before serving. Serve over ice. ◆Makes 5 servings.

Per serving: *Exchanges–1 fruit; Calories– 56; Carbohydrate–13.9 g*

PINEAPPLE AND YOGURT DIP

(Low fat/Low calorie) Get Me Out of the Kitchen Cookbook

1 cup nonfat vanilla yogurt
¼ cup flaked coconut
2 tablespoons packed brown sugar
1 (8 ounce) can crushed pineapple

In a medium size bowl, combine all ingredients. Mix well, cover and refrigerate 1 hour. ◆Makes 2 cups.

Per serving: *Calories–15; Protein–0g; Fat– 0mg; Carbohydrates–2 g; Cholesterol– 0mg; Sodium–5mg*

CREAMY ORANGE DIP

(Low fat/Low calorie)

1 (16 ounce) carton 1% cottage
  cheese
¼ cup nonfat yogurt
¼ teaspoon lemon juice
2 tablespoons frozen orange juice
1 teaspoon ground curry powder

In a blender container, combine all ingredients, cover and blend until smooth. Chill before serving. ◆Makes 20 servings.

Per serving (3 tablespoons each)**:** *Calories–21; Protein–3 g; Fat–0g; Carbohydrates–2 g; Sodium–95 mg*

Wild ponies have made their home at Assateague Island since they escaped shipwrecks of Spanish galleons and swum ashore. The Chinoteague National Wildlife Refuge in **Virginia** holds an annual pony roundup to keep the island from becoming overpopulated. The ponies swim across the channel, are herded down Main Street where some are sold at auction, then the others are swum back across to the island.

What will you trade for a ticket to see a theatrical production? Bob Porterfield asked that when he began the Barter Theatre in **Abingdon, Virginia,** in 1932 during the Great Depression. Pickles, pie, preserves, pigs and other food were traded for tickets. The actors had no money, but they ate well. It is still a thriving theatre today and draws over 150,000 tourists annually.

GREAT TASTING CRAB DIP
(Diabetic)

6 ounce fresh lump crabmeat
½ cup plain nonfat yogurt
⅓ cup reduced fat mayonnaise
1 tablespoon diced onion
2 teaspoons minced fresh parsley
2 teaspoons lemon juice
½ teaspoon Dijon mustard
¼ teaspoon dried dillweed

In a medium sized bowl, combine all ingredients, mix well. Cover and chill. ◆Makes 1½ cups.

Per tablespoon: *Exchange–Free; Calories–19; Carbohydrate–0.7g*

JUST A LITTLE BITE SALSA
(Diabetic)

1 large tomato, chopped
½ cup diced purple onion
⅛ teaspoon salt
1 (4 ounce) can chopped green chilies, undrained

In a medium bowl, combine all ingredients. Mix well. Cover and chill. ◆Makes 1¾ cups.

Per tablespoon: *Exchanges–free; Calories–4; Carbohydrates–1 g*

BURGER BITES

▼ *(Crock Pot—Low Fat/Low Cal)*

1 pound ground beef, cooked and drained
2 tablespoons ketchup
2 teaspoons instant minced onion
1 teaspoon mustard
2 cups cubed American cheese
24 miniature buns

Spray crock pot with vegetable spray. In crock pot, combine beef, ketchup, onion, and mustard mix well. Top with cheese. Cover and cook on low 3 to 4 hours. ◆Makes 24 appetizers.

Per serving: *Calories–170; Protein–8 g; Fat–8 g; Carbohydrate– 17 g; Sodium: 470 mg*

PARTY MEATBALLS

▼ *(Crock Pot—Low fat/ Low Cal)*

2 (8 ounce) packages frozen cooked meatballs
1 (12 ounce) jar savory beef gravy
1 (1 ounce) package dry onion soup mix

Place meatballs in crock pot. In medium bowl, combine gravy and onion soup mix, and mix well. Add mixture to meatballs. Cover; cook on low 3½ to 4½ hours. ◆Makes 72 meatballs.

Per serving (4 meatballs)**:** *Calories–170; Protein–10 g; Fat– 12 g; Carbohydrate–6 g; Cholesterol–30 mg; Sodium–510 mg*

The New River Gorge Bridge in **West Virginia** is the highest bridge east of the Mississippi River. Every year Bridge Day draws a large number of dare-devil parachutists who are allowed to jump from it on that day.

MIX IT & DIP IT

1 (8 ounce) package cream cheese

1 (16 ounce) bottle ranch salad dressing

3 tablespoons minced onion

1 celery stalk, diced

1 carrot, diced

In medium bowl, combine all ingredients. Mix well. Serve with crackers or chips. ◆Makes 6 servings.

Side Trips

The first Rand McNally map was published in 1872. They produced the first road map using numbered highways in 1917. Wisconsin was the first state to assign numbers and letters to roads. By 1922 Rand McNally had put markers along more than 50,000 miles of U.S. highways. They published their first Automobile Road Atlas in 1924.

Two states border eight other states. Tennessee borders Kentucky, Arkansas, Alabama, Georgia, Mississippi, Missouri, North Carolina, and Virginia. Missouri borders Tennessee, Arkansas, Kansas, Kentucky, Illinois, Iowa, Oklahoma, and Nebraska. Maine borders only New Hampshire.

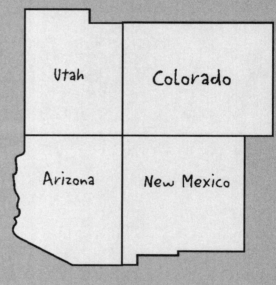

You can stand in four states at one time at Four Corners Monuments in the Southwest. It is the only place in the United States where four states have a common border: New Mexico, Arizona, Utah and Colorado.

A COOL DAY ASPARAGUS SOUP

1 tablespoon butter or margarine

1 small onion, chopped

2 (14½ ounce) cans chicken broth

1 (16 ounce) jar Alfredo sauce

2 (10 ounce) package frozen asparagus spears, thawed

In medium saucepan, combine butter and onion, cook over medium heat until tender. Stir in broth, Alfredo sauce, and asparagus spears. Bring to a boil. Reduce heat to low, simmer 5 minutes. Cool. Pour into blender, cover, blend until smooth. Return to pan, heat until hot. ◆Makes 8 servings.

CREAMY BROCCOLI SOUP

▼ *(Crock pot)*

1 small onion, chopped

1 tablespoon butter

1 (20 ounce) package of frozen broccoli

2 (10¾ ounce) cans cream of celery soup

1 (10¾ ounce) can cream of mushroom soup

1 cup grated American cheese

2 soup cans of milk

In medium skillet, sauté onion in butter over medium heat. Place in crock pot. Add broccoli, celery soup, mushroom soup, cheese, and milk. Cover and cook on low 3 to 4 hours. ◆Makes 6 to 8 servings.

CROCK POT BROCCOLI CHEESE SOUP

▼ *(Crock pot)*

1 (8 ounce) package Velveeta® cheese

2 (10¾ ounce) Cream of Celery soup

1 pint half and half milk

1 (10 ounce) package frozen chopped broccoli

In crock pot, combine all ingredients. Cover and cook on low 6 to 8 hours. ◆Makes 6 to 8 servings.

BROCCOLI CHEESE SOUP

▼ *(Crock pot)*

1 (10¾ ounce) can cheddar cheese soup

1 pint half and half

1 (10 ounce) package frozen chopped broccoli

In crock pot, combine all ingredients. Cover and cook on low 6 to 8 hours. ◆Makes 6 to 8 servings.

MIX UP
CHEDDAR CHEESE SOUP

2 (10¾ ounce) cans cheddar cheese soup

1½ cans water

½ cup chopped tomatoes

¼ cup green chilies

In medium saucepan, combine all ingredients. Cook over low heat until hot. ◆Makes 4 servings.

SLOW COOKED BROCCOLI CHEESE SOUP

▼ *(Crock pot)*

2 (16 ounce) package chopped broccoli

2 (10¾ ounce) cans cheddar cheese soup

2 (12 ounce) cans evaporated milk

¼ cup finely chopped onions

½ teaspoon salt

In crock pot, combine all ingredients. Cover and cook on low 6 to 8 hours. ◆Makes 8 servings.

QUICK LUNCH WITH SOUP

2 (10¾ ounce) cans cream of chicken soup

1 cup broccoli florets, thawed

1 cup cooked chicken cubes

1¾ cups milk

In medium saucepan, combine all ingredients. Heat over medium heat until hot. ◆Makes 4 servings.

The only state created by the Civil War and the only one resulting from presidential proclamation is **West Virginia.** By a two-thirds vote the state delegates opposed seceding from the Union, so President Abraham Lincoln issued a proclamation on April 20, 1863, that made West Virginia a state after 60 days.

From one extreme to another. In 1956 Cecil Underwood became **West Virginia's** youngest governor at the age of 34. In 1996 he was elected at age 77, making him the nation's oldest governor.

GET A GRIP ONION SOUP

▼ *(Crock pot – Low fat/Low cal)*

3 large onions, sliced

3 tablespoons butter or margarine, melted

3 tablespoons all-purpose flour

1 tablespoon Worcestershire sauce

1 teaspoon sugar

¼ teaspoon pepper

4 (14 ounce) cans beef broth

In crock pot, combine onions and butter. Cover and cook on high 35 minutes. In small bowl, combine flour, Worcestershire sauce, sugar, and pepper. Stir mixture and broth into onions. Cover and cook on low heat 7 to 9 hours. ◆Makes 8 servings.

Per serving: *Calories–190; Protein–10 gm; Fat–8 gm; Carbohydrates–21 gm; Cholesterol–10 mg; Sodium–1190 mg*

NEXT EXIT POTATO SOUP

4 medium potatoes, cooked and cubed
1 small onion, chopped
1 (10¾ ounce) can cheddar cheese soup
1 (10¾ ounce) can cream of celery soup
2 cups milk
1 teaspoon salt
½ teaspoon pepper

In large saucepan, combine all ingredients. Over low heat simmer 15 minutes. ◆Makes 4 to 6 servings.

ON THE GO POTATO SOUP

1 (16 ounce) package hash browns
1 small onion, chopped
2 cups water
1 (14 ounce) can chicken broth
1 (10¾ ounce) can cream of chicken soup
1 (10¾ ounce) cam cream of mushroom soup
2 cups milk

In large saucepan, combine hash browns, onions, water, and chicken broth. Over high heat bring to a boil. Reduce heat to low, cover and simmer 30 minutes. Add soups and milk. Simmer until well heated. Salt and pepper to taste. ◆Makes 6 to 8 servings.

The Breaks of the Big Sandy at Breaks Interstate Park is known as the Grand Canyon of the South. The Russell Fork of the Big Sandy River flows along the **Kentucky-Virginia** border through the Cumberland Mountains cutting a five mile long gorge that is 1,600 feet deep. The 46,000 acre park offers many sightseeing and recreational activities.

COLD DAY CHICKEN NOODLE SOUP

2 (10½ ounce) cans chicken broth
1 cup water
½ cup sliced carrots
½ cup sliced celery
1½ cup cooked, cubed chicken
1 cup uncooked medium egg noodles
1 tablespoon butter

In medium saucepan, combine broth, water, carrots, celery, and chicken. Cook over medium high heat to a boil. Stir in noodles. Reduce heat to medium. Cook 10 minutes or until noodles are done. Add butter. ◆Makes 4 servings.

GET THE CHILL OUT BEEF SOUP

1 (2.5 ounce) jar mushrooms
¼ green pepper, diced
1 tablespoon butter or margarine
1 (10¾ ounce) can beef soup
2 (10¾ ounce) cans beef noodle soup
1½ cans water

In large saucepan, brown mushrooms and pepper in butter over medium heat. Add soups and water. Bring to a boil. Turn heat to low, simmer 15 minutes. ◆Makes 4 to 6 servings.

VEGGIE BEEF SOUP

(Low fat/Low cal)

½ pound extra lean ground beef

1 (14 ounce) can ready to serve beef broth

1 (14.5 ounce) can stewed tomatoes, chopped, undrained

1 cup frozen mixed vegetables

1 (8 ounce) can no salt tomato sauce

⅓ cup uncooked quick cooking barley

In large skillet, brown ground beef over medium heat, drain. Add beef broth, stewed tomatoes, vegetables, tomato sauce, and barley. Bring to a boil. Reduce heat to low, cook for 15 minutes. ◆Makes 4 - 1½ cup servings.

Per serving: *Calories–210; Protein–15 gm; Fat–8 gm; Carbohydrates–19 gm; Cholesterol–35 mg; Sodium–640 mg*

The president of the Confederate States of America was born in **Fairview, Kentucky.** A monument was erected in Jefferson Davis' hometown. At 351 feet high, it is the fourth tallest in the country and the tallest made of cast concrete. An Elevator will take you to the top for a view of the surrounding countryside. His opponent, Abraham Lincoln, was also born in Kentucky.

U.S. President David Rice Atchison was born in **Fayette County, Kentucky,** (near Lexington). Never heard of him? He was president for one day. President James K. Polk's last day of office was on a Saturday, and Zachary Taylor, the President-elect refused to be sworn in on a Sunday, March 4, 1849. With no president or vice president in office, the presidency fell to Atchison, the president pro-tem of the Senate.

NO FUSS VEGGIE BEEF SOUP

▼*(Crock pot)*

1 pound ground beef, browned and drained

2 cups tomato juice

2 cups beef broth

1 (16 ounce) package frozen mixed vegetables

In crock pot, combine all ingredients. Cover and cook on low 3 to 4 hours. ◆Makes 4 to 5 servings.

REST STOP
BEEF BARLEY SOUP

(Low fat/Low cal)

½ pound extra lean ground beef, cooked and drained

1 (14.5 ounce) can stewed tomatoes, chopped

1 cup frozen mixed vegetables

1 (8 ounce) can no salt added tomato sauce

⅓ cup uncooked quick cooking barley

In large saucepan, combine all ingredients. Bring to a boil, over medium heat. Cover and cook 15 minutes or until vegetables are tender. ◆Makes 4 – 1½ cup servings.

Per serving: *Calories–210; Protein–7 gm; Fat–9 gm; Carbohydrates–11 gm; Cholesterol–30 mg; Sodium–170 mg*

GOLD COAST OYSTER SOUP

¼ cup butter or margarine
½ cup thinly sliced green onion
2 tablespoons flour
2 cups half and half
2 cups shucked fresh oysters and their liquid

Melt butter in 3 quart saucepan over medium heat. Add green onions and cook 5 minutes. Add flour; cook 1 minute, stirring constantly. Gradually stir in half and half until smooth. Heat to broiling, stirring constantly. Add oysters and liquid. Cook until soup thickens. ◆Makes 4 servings.

ON THE ROAD CLAM CHOWDER

2 (10¾ ounce) cans clam chowder soup
1 cup corn
2½ cups chopped cooked shrimp
1¾ cup milk

In medium saucepan, combine all ingredients. Simmer on low heat 15 minutes, stirring often. ◆Makes 4 servings.

Remember that Corvette you dreamed of owning? More than 50 Corvettes are displayed at the National Corvette Museum in **Bowling Green, Kentucky.** It is just down the road from the Corvette plant where every U.S. made Corvette is manufactured.

BAYSIDE CLAM CHOWDER

▼ *(Crock pot)*

3 (10 ¾ ounce) cans cream of potato soup

2 (10 ¾ ounce) cans clam chowder soup

½ cup butter

1 small onion, diced

1 pint half and half

2 (6 ½ ounce) cans clams, chopped

In crock pot, combine all ingredients. Cover and cook on low 3 to 4 hours. ◆Makes 4 to 6 servings.

HAM AND BUTTER BEANS SOUP

1 pound butter beans

1 teaspoon salt

½ cup butter

1 cup cubed ham

In large saucepan, add beans and salt; cover with water until half full, cover. Over medium heat, cook 1½ hours, add water when needed. Add butter and ham. Cook for 20 minutes. ◆Makes 6 to 8 servings.

FLORIDA ORANGE SALAD

1½ pounds sea scallops, cut in half
½ teaspoon salt
4 cups torn into bite size, spinach
2 kiwifruit, peeled and sliced
2 medium oranges, peeled and sliced

In 2 quart casserole, combine scallops and salt. Cover and microwave on high 6 to 9 minutes or until done. Drain, cover and chill. Add spinach and fruit. Drizzle with Florida orange salad dressing. ◆Makes 4 servings.

Florida Orange Salad Dressing

1 teaspoon grated orange peel
¼ cup orange juice
2 tablespoons vegetable oil
2 tablespoons lemon juice
½ teaspoon sugar

In container, combine all ingredients. Shake well.

Berea College in **Kentucky** was founded in 1855 for students, mainly from Appalachia, who could not afford to go to college. Students were (and are) required to work to pay their tuition. Various crafts were part of the work activities, so Berea became a craft center. Berea College was the first interracial college south of the Mason-Dixon line.

The town of **Middlesboro, Kentucky,** is built within a meteor crater. Over 300 million years ago, the celestial visitor struck the earth and left a crater almost four miles in diameter.

LIME FLUFFY SALAD

1 (4 ounce) box lime gelatin

2 cups cottage cheese

1 (14 ounce) can crushed pineapple, drained

1 (6 ounce) carton whip topping

In large bowl, combine all ingredients. Mix well and chill. ◆Makes 6 servings.

SUNNY PEACH SALAD

1 (20 ounce) can crushed pineapple with juice

2 (4 serving) boxes peach Jell-O®

2 cups buttermilk

1 (8 ounce) tub whip topping

In medium saucepan, combine pineapple with juice and peach Jell-O®. Heat over medium heat until hot. Cool. Add buttermilk and whip topping, mix well. Cover and chill. ◆Makes 6 to 8 servings.

SPICE IT UP APPLE SALAD

1 cup hot water
¼ cup red hots
2 teaspoons sugar
1 (4 serving) box cherry Jell-O®
1 cup cold water
1 cup diced apples
¼ cup chopped pecans

In medium saucepan, combine water, red hots, and sugar. Heat over high heat until boiling. Add cherry Jell-O®. Stir until Jell-O® dissolves. Add cold water. Chill until almost firm. Add apples and pecans. Chill until firm.

JELL-O TWIST SALAD

1 (4 serving) box any flavor Jell-O®
1 (16 ounce) carton cottage cheese
1 (8 ounce) can crushed pineapple
1 (8 ounce) tub frozen whip topping

In medium bowl, sprinkle dry Jell-O® over cottage cheese. Add pineapple, mix well. Fold in whip topping and chill. ◆Makes 6 to 8 servings.

America's most completely restored Shaker community is at **Pleasant Hill, Kentucky,** near Harrodsburg. There are 34 original 19TH century buildings and 2,800 acres of farmland on the National Historic Land-mark. Men and women lived separately and practiced celi-bacy. They took in orphans and depended upon converts to keep their order alive. They were very industrious and were noted for their crafts, especially furniture.

ORANGE FRUIT SALAD

(Diabetic)

2 medium oranges, peeled, sectioned, seeded

1 medium red delicious apple, chopped

2 medium carrots, shredded

½ stalk of celery, thinly sliced

¼ cup raisins

2 tablespoons reduced fat mayonnaise

½ teaspoon lemon juice

In medium bowl, combine oranges, apple, carrots, celery, and raisins, toss. Add mayonnaise and lemon juice. Mix until well coated. Cover and chill. ◆Makes 4 – ½ cup servings.

Per serving: *Exchanges–2 vegetable, 1 fruit, ½ fat; Calories– 115; Carbohydrates–24.5*

ANYTIME FRUIT SALAD

1 (8 ounce) tub whip topping

1 (14 ounce) can sweetened condensed milk

1 (20 ounce) can cherry pie filling

1 (20 ounce) can crushed pineapple, drained

2 cups miniature marshmallows

1 cup walnuts

In large bowl, combine whip topping and milk. Mix well. Fold in cherry pie filling and pineapple. Add marshmallows and nuts. Mix well. Cover and chill. ◆Makes 6 to 8 servings.

A HOT DAY FRUIT SALAD

1 medium apple, unpeeled, chopped
2 medium carrots, chopped
3 medium oranges, peeled, chopped
½ cup raisins
¾ cup Miracle Whip®
1 tablespoon sugar

In large bowl, combine all ingredients. Cover and chill. Serve on lettuce leaves. ◆Makes 4 servings.

SASSY FRUIT SALAD

½ cup honey
½ cup frozen (thawed) limeade concentrate
1 teaspoon sugar
8 cups cut up fresh fruit

In large bowl, combine honey, limeade, and sugar. Mix well. Add fruit and toss. ◆Makes 8 servings.

Harrodsburg, Kentucky, is the oldest permanent white settlement west of the Allegheny Mountains. Boonesboro, founded earlier by famed frontiersman, Daniel Boone, was located too near the Kentucky River and was subject to periodic flooding which kept it from thriving. Both Ft. Harrod and Ft. Boonesboro are Kentucky State Parks.

At **Blowing Rock, North Carolina,** a strong updraft at a rock ledge overhanging the John's River Gorge will usually return items (such as a handkerchief) that are tossed over the ledge. According to Indian folklore, a maiden prayed to the God of the Winds to return her warrior, who had fallen over. The wind came up and blew him back.

CRANBERRY FREEZE SALAD

1 (16 ounce) can cranberry sauce

1 (8 ounce) can crushed pineapple

1 (8 ounce) tub whip topping

2 (3 ounce) package cream cheese

2 tablespoons mayonnaise

1 cup chopped pecans

In medium bowl, combine all ingredients and freeze. ◆Makes 6 to 8 servings.

NEW YORK FRUIT SALAD

1 (16 ounce) carton of whipping cream

1 (8 ounce) can crushed pineapple, drained

1 (6 ounce) jar maraschino cherries, drained, halved

2 bananas, chopped

¾ cup small marshmallows

1 tablespoon confectioners sugar

2 tablespoons mayonnaise

In large bowl, whip cream; fold in pineapple, cherries, bananas, and marshmallows. In small bowl, combine sugar and mayonnaise, add to fruit mixture. Pour into 9x10 inch pan and freeze. Cut into squares and serve on lettuce leaves. ◆Makes 6 to 8 servings.

CASUAL GET TOGETHER APPLE SALAD

2 cups diced apples
1 cup diced celery
⅓ cup chopped nuts
½ cup Miracle Whip®
1 teaspoon sugar

In medium bowl, combine all ingredients. Mix well. Serve on crisp lettuce. ◆Makes 4 servings.

EVERYDAY CABBAGE SLAW

2 cup shredded green cabbage
1 cup shredded red cabbage
½ cup shredded carrots

Dressing

¼ cup Miracle Whip®
2 teaspoons sugar
2 teaspoons cider vinegar

In large bowl, combine cabbage and carrots. Mix well. In small bowl, combine Miracle Whip, sugar, and vinegar. Pour over cabbage. Mix well and chill. ◆Makes 6 servings.

BUSHMAN GREEN BEAN SALAD

2 cups fresh green beans, cooked but firm
½ small onion, sliced
2 tablespoons salad oil
¾ tablespoon wine vinegar

In medium bowl, combine all ingredients. Mix well and chill.
◆Makes 4 servings.

UPDATED PEA SALAD

(Low fat/Low cal)

¼ cup whipping cream
¼ cup sour cream
½ teaspoon Dijon mustard
2 teaspoons finely chopped fresh sage
¼ teaspoon grated lemon peel
¼ teaspoon salt
¼ teaspoon pepper
3 cups frozen sweet peas, cooked, cooled
2 ounces cheddar cheese, diced

In medium bowl, combine whipping cream, sour cream, mustard, sage, lemon peel, salt, and pepper. Mix well. Add peas and cheese, mix, cover, and chill. ◆Makes 6 – ½ cup servings.

Per serving: *Calories–150; Protein–7 gm; Fat–9 gm; Carbohydrates–11 gm; Cholesterol–30 mg; Sodium–170 mg*

CUT TO THE CHASE PEA SALAD

¾ cup cooked peas

¼ cup diced cheddar cheese

1 tablespoon diced onion

2½ tablespoons Miracle Whip®

2 tablespoons diced celery

½ teaspoon sugar

In medium bowl, combine all ingredients and chill. ◆Makes 2 servings.

A CRUNCHY PEA SALAD

1 (10 ounce) package frozen green peas, uncooked

1½ cup Spanish nuts

½ cup Miracle Whip®

½ cup sour cream

1 tablespoon lemon juice

1 teaspoon Worcestershire sauce

In medium bowl, combine all ingredients. Mix well. Cover and chill. Serve on crisp lettuce. ◆Makes 4 to 6 servings.

The Nantahala Gorge in the small range of Nantahala Mountains between the Blue Ridge and Smoky Mountains in Western **North Carolina** is so deep and narrow that only at midday does the sun strike the bottom. Indian legend says that it was inhabited by a horned dragon or serpent that had a jewel in the center of its forehead and put a curse upon anyone who looked upon it. A Cherokee brave killed the monster and took the jewel, which was supposed to reveal the future to its possessor.

Blackbeard the Pirate sailed the water of the Outer Banks of **North Carolina** and often took his ship into Ocracoke on Pimlico Sound. He had friends in Edenton on Albemarle Sound and near here Lt. Robert Maynard tracked down and defeated Blackbeard.

SOUTHWEST SALAD

(Diabetic)

1 (15 ounce) can no salt added black beans, drained and rinsed

¼ cup chopped green onion

½ cup salsa

2 cups shredded romaine lettuce

In medium bowl, combine beans, onion, and salsa. Mix well. Spoon mixture over lettuce. ◆Makes 4 servings.

Per serving: *Exchanges–1 starch, 1 vegetable; Calories–111; Carbohydrates–21.3 gm*

ON THE MOVE SPINACH SALAD

(Diabetic)

1 (10 ounce) package torn fresh spinach

1 cup croutons

1 tablespoon crumbled bacon bits

½ cup fat free sweet and sour dressing

In large bowl, combine spinach, croutons, and bacon bits. Toss well. Add dressing, mix well. ◆Makes 6½ cup servings.

Per serving: *Exchanges–1 starch; Calories–77; Carbohydrates–13.5 gm*

WEEKDAY MACARONI SALAD

1 cup macaroni, cooked
½ cup shredded cheddar cheese
2 stalks celery, diced
2 green onions, chopped
¾ cup Miracle Whip®

In medium bowl, combine all ingredients. Mix well and chill. ◆Makes 2 to 3 servings.

TASTY RICE SALAD

1 cup cooked rice
1 cup small marshmallows
1 cup pineapple tidbits
½ cup coconut
2 apples, diced
1½ cups whip topping

In medium bowl, combine all ingredients. Cover and chill. ◆Makes 4 to 6 servings.

The **Beaufort, North Carolina,** Old Burying Ground, dating from 1731, supposedly has an English soldier buried standing up because he swore he would never lie down on foreign soil. There's also a little girl buried in a barrel of rum. She died at sea. Her father had promised her mother when they left that he would bring her back. Embalming her in rum was the only way he could keep his promise.

In 1587 the English tried to establish the first colony in the New World at **Roanoke Island, North Carolina.** Sir Walter Raleigh sailed to England for supplies, but was detained. When he returned three years later the people had vanished and there were no signs of what had happened to them. "The Lost Colony," an outdoor drama, tells the story each summer. One of Andy Griffith's first acting roles was as Sir Walter Raleigh in the drama.

PICNIC TIME POTATO SALAD

4 potatoes, cooked, cubed

3 hard boiled eggs, chopped

1 small onion, chopped

2 celery stalks, chopped

1¾ cups Miracle Whip®

1 tablespoon sugar

¼ cup pickle relish

In large bowl, combine all ingredients. Mix well. Cover and chill. ◆Makes 6 to 8 servings.

CALIFORNIA CHICKEN SALAD

4 chicken breast, cooked, cubed

½ cup Miracle Whip®

⅓ cup milk

1 teaspoon sugar

2 celery stalks, thinly sliced

4 medium oranges peeled, seeded, sectioned

In large bowl, place chicken. In small bowl, combine Miracle Whip, milk, and sugar. Mix well. Pour mixture over chicken. Add celery and oranges, toss well. Line salad plates with lettuce, spoon chicken mixture on plates. ◆Makes 6 servings.

SHOWING OFF
CHICKEN SALAD

(Diabetic)

2 cups low sodium chicken broth

2 boneless, skinless chicken breast,
   10 to 12 ounces

½ small red onion, minced

4 medium stalks celery minced

¼ cup low fat sour cream

¼ cup nonfat mayonnaise

2 teaspoons crushed dried tarragon

¼ teaspoon white pepper

In medium saucepan with chicken broth, place chicken breast. Cook over medium heat 15 minutes. Remove chicken and cool. Cut chicken into bite size pieces. In a medium bowl, combine chicken, onion, celery, sour cream, mayonnaise, tarragon, and white pepper. Mix well. Serve on 4 plates with lettuce. ◆Makes 4 servings.

Per serving: *Exchanges–2 lean meat, 1 vegetable; Calories–128; Carbohydrates–5 gm*

Don't go to Scotland to see the Loch Ness Monster. Many residents of **Irmo, South Carolina,** claim to have seen a local version which they call the Loch Murray Monster. It is supposedly a cross between a snake and something prehistoric.

A beautiful Cherokee maiden named Falling Rock loved and was to marry a handsome young brave from a distant village. He disappeared on a hunting trip, never to be seen again. The heart-broken woman spent the rest of her life searching for her missing brave. Legend has it that to this day she still roams the Great Smoky Mountains searching for her one true love. In fact, as you travel this area of **Tennessee** and **North Carolina** you may see signs that say, "Watch for Falling Rock."

DELAWARE CHICKEN SALAD

3 cups chicken, cooked, cubed
3 hard cooked eggs, chopped
1 teaspoon salt
1 cup diced celery
3 sweet pickles, chopped
¾ cup Miracle Whip®

In medium bowl, combine all ingredients. Mix well. Cover and chill. ◆Makes 4 to 6 servings.

VERMONT PEPPERONI SALAD

1 (16 ounce) package broccoli, red peppers, onion, and mushrooms
2 cups cooked macaroni
1 (3 ounce) package pepperoni
½ cup ranch salad dressing

In medium saucepan, cook vegetables according to package directions, drain. In a large bowl, combine vegetables, and macaroni. Chill. Add pepperoni and dressing. Mix well. Add salt and pepper to taste. ◆Makes 4 to 6 servings.

TUNA SCOOP SALAD

1 (6 ounce) can tuna, drained

1 cup chopped celery

1 cup finely shredded cabbage

¾ cup Miracle Whip®

1 teaspoon sugar

In medium bowl, combine tuna, celery, and cabbage. Mix well. In small bowl combine Miracle Whip® and sugar. Pour over tuna mixture and mix well. Scoop mixture on 6 plates with lettuce leaves. ◆Makes 6 servings.

HONEY LIME DRESSING

1 tablespoon lime juice

1 tablespoon honey

½ teaspoon cornstarch

⅛ teaspoon poppy seed

In small microwave bowl, combine all ingredients. Micro-wave on high 30 to 40 seconds or until mixture thickens. ◆Makes 2 servings.

IT WORKS SALAD DRESSING

1 cup Miracle Whip®

¼ cup milk

1 teaspoon sugar

In small bowl, combine all ingredients. Cover and chill 30 minutes. ◆Makes 1¼ cups.

Lookout Mountain in southeastern **Tennessee** near Chattanooga has a cave which contains Ruby Falls, the highest underground waterfall in the United States, 145 feet. Ruby Falls is 1,120 feet underground.

4 STEP SALAD DRESSING

(Low fat/Low cal)

2 cups buttermilk

2 tablespoons Dijon mustard

3 tablespoons coarse mustard

1 tablespoon frozen apple juice, thawed

In a medium bowl, combine all ingredients. Mix well. Cover, and chill. ◆Makes 2 – ½ cup servings.

Per serving (1 tablespoon): *Calories–9; Protein–1 gm; Fat–0; Carbohydrates–1 gm; Sodium–65 mg*

SHORT CUT YOGURT DRESSING

1 cup yogurt

2 tablespoons Miracle Whip®

1 teaspoon sugar

⅛ teaspoon lemon juice

In small bowl, combine all ingredients. Mix well. Cover and chill. ◆Makes 1¼ cups.

THOUSAND ISLAND DRESSING

1 cup Miracle Whip®

½ cup catsup

2 tablespoons sweet relish

1 hard boiled egg, finely chopped

In small bowl, combine all ingredients. Mix well and chill. ◆Makes 1½ cups.

A NIFTY SALAD DRESSING

1 (10¾ ounce) can tomato soup

1 cup salad oil

¼ cup sugar

½ cup vinegar

⅛ teaspoon garlic salt

In medium bowl, combine all ingredients. Pour in 1 quart fruit jar, cover and shake. Chill. ◆Makes 3 cups.

BLUE CHEESE DRESSING

3 ounces blue cheese, crumbled

1 cup sour cream

1 cup Miracle Whip®

2 teaspoons soy sauce

1 clove garlic, minced

Juice of 1 lemon

In medium bowl, combine all ingredients. Mix well. Cover and chill. ◆Makes 2½ cups.

Reelfoot Lake in northwest **Tennessee** was formed when the Mississippi River flowed backwards. An earthquake in December, 1911, caused great bluffs to topple into the Mississippi and Ohio Rivers and tilted the bed of the Mississippi so that it flowed upstream. The surface of a thick forest fell 8 feet and the waters rushed in to form the lake. It is 18 miles long and up to 3 miles wide.

HOLLANDAISE SAUCE

½ cup butter

2 egg yokes

¼ teaspoon salt

½ cup boiling water

1 tablespoon lemon juice

In small bowl, combine butter, egg yolks, and salt. Mix well. Add boiling water and stir until right consistency. Add lemon juice, stirring rapidly. Serve with asparagus, broccoli, or fish. ◆Makes 1½ cups.

Pedal to the Metal

In 1900 there were 144 miles of surfaced roads in the United States. Now there are over three million miles.

President Dwight D. Eisenhower championed the cause of the Interstate Highway System of major roads connecting all our cities, inaugurated in 1956. He wanted one mile out of five to be laid out straight for airplanes to use in case of war or emergency. I-90 from Seattle to Boston is the longest—3,085.27 miles. I-97 from Annapolis to Baltimore is the shortest–17.5 miles.

The nation's most famous road is Route 66, also known as the "Mother Road." It was the first major highway crossing much of the country, going from Chicago to Santa Monica, California, 2,448 miles. It was dedicated in 1926 and was paved 11 years later.

MAD MAX BEEF BURGERS

1 (10¾ ounce) can gumbo soup
¼ cup ketchup
1 tablespoon mustard
1½ pounds ground beef, browned
1 teaspoon salt
½ teaspoon pepper

In large saucepan, combine all ingredients. Cook over medium heat 5 minutes. Reduce heat to low, simmer 10 minutes. ◆Makes 4 to 6 servings.

SHOWING OFF CHEESEBURGERS

3 pounds ground beef
½ cup dry bread crumbs
2 eggs
1 teaspoon salt
1¼ cups shredded cheese

In large bowl, combine beef, bread crumbs, eggs, and salt. Mix well but lightly. Divide mixture into 24 balls. Flatten each ball to 4 inches across. Place 1 tablespoon cheese on 12 patties. Top with remaining patties. Press edges to seal. Grill patties 6 to 8 minutes on each side, turning only once. ◆Makes 12 servings.

The quaint little village of **Bell Buckle, Tennessee,** is home of Webb School, a preparatory school that has produced ten Rhodes Scholars and governors of three states. The original wood-shingled one room schoolhouse built in 1870, complete with potbelled stove is open to the public. Bell Buckle is also home of the Louvin Brothers, stars of the Grand Ole Opry.

The Alvin York State Historical Area north of **Jamestown, Tennessee,** commemorates the life and career of one of America's most celebrated heroes. Sgt. York spent all his life except the two war years in these mountains. In October, 1918 he killed 25 German soldiers and almost single-handedly captured another 132. He received more than 40 Allied decorations.

NORTH DAKOTA GRILLED BURGERS

1½ pounds ground beef

1½ cups shredded cheddar cheese

3 tablespoons chopped green onions

1 teaspoon salt

In large bowl, combine all ingredients. Mix well. Shape mixture into 6 patties. Place on grill. Cook 4 to 6 inches from heat, until desired doneness. ◆Makes 6 servings.

GRILLED ONION BURGERS

1 pound ground beef

½ cup diced onions

½ teaspoon salt

½ teaspoon pepper

1 teaspoon Worcestershire sauce

In medium bowl, combine all ingredients. Mix well. Make 4 patties. Grill 5 to 6 inches from heat, until desired doneness. ◆Makes 4 servings.

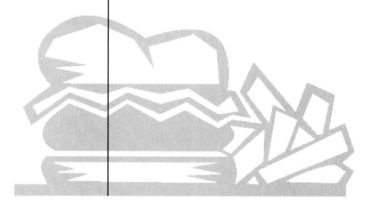

SPEED TRAP BURGERS

1 pound sausage

2 (2 pounds) ground beef

2 tablespoons Worcestershire sauce

2 tablespoons minced onion

In large bowl, combine all ingredients. Mix well. Form into patties. Grill or cook in skillet until well done. ◆Makes 10 servings.

AMERICA'S FAVORITE POT ROAST

▼ *(Crock pot)*

1 teaspoon salt

½ teaspoon pepper

3 to 4 pounds chuck roast

2 tablespoons oil

½ cup flour

4 medium potatoes, cut in quarters

3 carrots, sliced

2 stalks celery, sliced

1 medium onion, sliced

½ cup hot water

Salt and pepper roast. Dredge roast in flour. In large skillet with oil, heat over medium heat. Brown roast. In crock pot, put vegetables. Add roast and water. Cover and cook on low 10 to 12 hours. ◆Makes 6 to 8 servings.

CROCK POT CHUCK ROAST

3 to 4 pounds beef chuck roast
2 tablespoons oil
⅓ cup creamy horseradish
½ cup water

In large skillet, brown roast in oil over medium heat. In crock pot, place roast. Spread top of roast with horseradish. Add water. Cover and cook on low 8 to 10 hours. ◆Makes 6 to 8 servings.

ROUTE 66 POT ROAST

▼ *(Crock pot)*

1 (10¾ ounce) can cream of mushroom soup
1 (1 ounce) envelope dry onion soup
¼ cup water
3¼ to 4 pounds chuck pot roast

In medium bowl, combine onion soup and water. Mix well. In crock pot, place roast. Pour mixture over roast. Cover and cook on low 8 to 9 hours. ◆Makes 8 servings.

MIX AND FORGET IT ROAST

▼ *(Crock pot)*

3 pounds roast
2 (⅞ ounce) envelope brown gravy mix
1½ cups water

In crock pot, place roast. In medium bowl, combine gravy mix and water. Mix well. Pour gravy mixture over roast. Cover and cook on high 6 to 8 hours. If frozen 8 to 10 hours. ◆Makes 6 servings.

BARBECUE SPARERIBS

▼ *(Crock pot)*

3 to 4 pounds spareribs

1 large onion, sliced

1 (24 ounce) bottle barbecue sauce

In crock pot, place spareribs. Top with onions. Pour barbecue sauce over onions. Cover and cook on high 1½ hours. Turn to low and cook 8 hours. ◆Makes 4 to 6 serving.

FORK TENDER SHORT RIBS

▼ *(Crock pot)*

4 pounds beef short ribs

1 medium onion, sliced

1 (12 ounce) jar beef gravy

1 (1¼ ounce) envelope beef gravy mix

In crock pot, place ribs, cover with onions. In a medium bowl, combine gravy and dry gravy mix. Pour over top. Cover and cook on low 9 to 11 hours. ◆Makes 6 servings.

The "Granite Capital of the World" is **Elberton, Georgia.** About forty-five granite quarries operate in this northeast Georgia area and produce more granite monuments than any other place in the world.

The first person to use ether as an anesthetic during an operation was Dr. Crawford W. Long of **Jefferson, Georgia.** In 1842 he used sulfuric ether as an anesthetic before removing a tumor from a man's neck.

WYOMING OH SO DELICIOUS BEEF

▼ *(Crockpot)*

3 to 4 pounds chuck beef roast

1 (6 ounce) jar sliced dill pickles, undrained

1 medium onion, chopped

1 teaspoon mustard seed

4 garlic cloves, chopped

1 (14 ounce) can crushed tomatoes with Italian seasoning

In crock pot, place roast. Pour pickles with juice over top of beef. Add onions, mustard seed, garlic, and tomatoes. Cover and cook on low 8 to 10 hours. Shred beef. Pile beef onto toasted roll or buns. ◆Makes 6 to 8 servings.

TEXAS T-BONE

6 beef T-bone steaks, 1 inch thick

3 cloves garlic, cut in half

salt

pepper

Trim fat from steaks. Rub garlic on both sides of steaks. Grill over direct heat 10 to 15 minutes for medium doneness. Salt and pepper to taste. ◆Makes 6 servings.

CONNECTICUT SWISS STEAK

▼ *(Crock pot)*

4 pounds top sirloin steaks, cut in serving size

2 (14½ ounce) can diced tomatoes

2 green bell peppers, sliced into ½ inch strips

1 medium onion, chopped

1½ teaspoons salt

1 teaspoon pepper

In crock pot, place steak. Add tomatoes, bell pepper, onion, salt, and pepper. Cover and cook on low 8 hours. ◆Makes 10 servings.

A ROBUST BEEF BRISKET

▼ *(Crock pot)*

3 to 3½ pounds trimmed corn beef brisket

¾ teaspoon crushed red pepper

1 cup reduced sodium chicken broth

1 tablespoon Worcestershire sauce

In crock pot, place beef. Sprinkle red pepper over beef. In small bowl, combine broth and Worcestershire sauce. Pour over beef. Cover and cook on low 8 to 9 hours. ◆Makes 8 servings.

Civic pride can accomplish a lot. Business men in **Helen, Georgia,** decided their little town was bleak and could stand some improvement. A local artist did water color sketches of an Alpine Helen. People began renovating their shops, utilities went underground, and the city put up quaint street lights. It is now a picture book Bavarian Village.

On Sunday, March 7, 1965, several hundred blacks attempted to cross the Edmund Pettis Bridge in **Selma, Alabama,** on the start of a proposed march to the state capitol. They were making a stand for the rights of all Americans, regardless of color, to vote. They were set upon by a battalion of state troopers with clubs and tear gas. The carnage and the demonstrators' nonviolent lack of resistance were broadcast across nation. Bloody Sunday led to Congress passing the Voting Rights Act of 1965. The National Voting Rights Museum is near the bridge.

MIX IT QUICK MEAT LOAF

2 pounds ground beef

2 eggs

1 package saltine crackers, crushed

1 small onion, chopped

2 cups salsa

Preheat oven to 350 degrees. In large bowl, combine beef, eggs, crackers, onion, and 1 cup salsa. Mix well. Shape mixture into 9x5x2 inch loaf pan. Pour 1 cup salsa on top of mixture. Bake uncovered 1½ hours. ◆Makes 6 servings.

MEXI MEATLOAF

▼*(Crock pot)*

2 pounds ground beef

2 cups crushed corn chips

1 cup grated cheddar cheese

⅔ cup salsa

4 teaspoons taco seasoning

2 eggs, beaten

In large bowl, combine all ingredients. Mix well. shape mixture into a loaf. Place in crock pot. Cover and cook on low 8 to 10 hours. ◆Makes 4 to 6 servings.

QUICK BEEF TOPPER

▼ *(Crockpot)*

2 pounds beef, cubed

2 (10¾ ounce) cans cream of mushroom soup

1 (4 ounce) can mushrooms, with liquid

½ cup wine

In crockpot, combine all ingredients. Cover; cook on low 7 to 8 hours. Serve over rice or noodles. Makes 4 to 6 servings.

SAUSAGE TOPPER FOR FETTUCCINI

1 pound fully cooked polish sausage, cut into ½ inch pieces

2 (15 ounce) cans chunky garlic and herb tomato sauce

1 (16 ounce) package frozen stir fry bell pepper and onion, thawed

In large saucepan, combine all ingredients. Heat mixture over medium heat to boiling. Reduce heat to low, simmer 5 minutes. Serve mixture over cooked fettuccine. ◆Makes 4 servings.

CORNED BEEF RUEBENS

▼ *(Crock pot)*

2 to 3 pounds marinated corn beef

2 garlic cloves, minced

10 peppercorns

In crock pot, place corned beef. Top with garlic and peppercorns. Cover and cook on high 4 to 5 hours. To make Rueben sandwiches, slice corned beef thin, use pumpernickel bread, Swiss cheese, sauerkraut, and thousand island dressing on each sandwich. ◆Makes 6 servings.

OKLAHOMA CHICKEN FRIED STEAK

2 eggs
¼ cup milk
1 teaspoon salt
1 teaspoon pepper
1½ to 2 pounds tenderized steak, cut in serving size
¼ cup oil

In small bowl, combine eggs, milk, salt, and pepper. Put flour in separate shallow pan. Dredge each piece of steak in flour and then dip in egg mixture. Dip again in flour. In large skillet, heat oil over medium heat until hot. Place steaks in skillet, brown on both sides. Reduce heat to low. Cover and cook 10 to 15 minutes. ◆Makes 4 to 6 servings.

PORK CHOPS THAT SIZZLE

1 tablespoon chili powder
1 teaspoon ground cumin
¼ teaspoon ground red pepper
1 clove garlic, diced
8 pork chops, ½ inch thick

In small bowl, combine chili powder, cumin, red pepper, and garlic. Mix well. Rub mixture evenly on both sides of chops. Chill one hour. Grill 4 to 5 inches from heat 12 to 15 minutes, turning frequently. ◆Makes 8 servings.

SIDE OF THE ROAD PORK CHOPS

1 (1 ounce) envelope onion soup mix
½ cup plain dry bread crumbs
4 pork chops, 1 inch thick
2 eggs, beaten

Preheat oven to 400 degrees. In small bowl, combine soup mix and bread crumbs. Dip chops in egg, then in bread crumb mixture, until evenly coated. In a greased 13x9 inch baking pan, arrange chops. Bake uncovered 25 minutes or until done. ◆Make 4 servings.

ILLINOIS KRAUT CHOPS

▼ *(Crock pot)*

3 pounds pork chops
½ teaspoon garlic powder
½ teaspoon pepper
1 (32 ounce) bag sauerkraut
1 cup applesauce

In crock pot, place chops. Sprinkle with garlic powder and pepper. Pour sauerkraut and then applesauce over chops. Cover and cook on low 6 to 8 hours. ◆Makes 6 to 8 servings.

Houston and Florida get all the attention, but there wouldn't be a space program if it weren't for **Huntsville, Alabama.** Werner Von Braun, German V–2 rocket scientist, came to Huntsville in 1950 to produce the Redstone Rocket. The U.S. Space and Rocket Center there features near its entrance a full scale replica of the 363 feet, three stage, Saturn V, the rocket that took man to the moon.

The dining room walls of the Cabbage Key Inn and Restaurant in **Cabbage Key, Florida,** are made of money. They are covered with one dollar bills held in place with masking tape. Each of the more than $10,000 worth of dollar bills are signed by the tourist who put it there.

PIZZA TASTING PORK CHOPS

▼ *(Crock pot)*

2 tablespoons oil

6 pork chops, 1 inch thick, fat removed

2 cups pizza sauce

½ teaspoon dried basil leaves

½ teaspoon salt

1 small onion, chopped

In large skillet with oil, brown pork chops over medium heat. Place browned pork chops in crock pot. In medium bowl, combine pizza sauce, dried basil, salt, and onion. Mix well. Pour mixture over chops. Cover and cook on low 5 to 6 hours. ◆Makes 6 servings.

IOWA FRIED PORK CHOPS

1 teaspoon salt

1 teaspoon pepper

6 pork chops, 1 inch thick

½ cup flour

¼ cup oil

Salt and pepper chops. Dredge chops in flour. In large skillet with oil, heat over medium high heat, brown chops. Reduce heat to low and cook 10 to 15 minutes. ◆Makes 6 servings.

IN A HURRY PORK CHOPS
▼ *(Crockpot)*

4 pork chops
1 (16 ounce) bottle Italian dressing

In crockpot, place pork chops. Pour dressing over chops. Cover; cook on high 6 to 8 hours. ◆Makes 4 servings.

CELERY AROUND PORK CHOPS
▼ *(Crock pot)*

6 pork chops, 1 inch thick
1 (10¾ ounce) can cream of celery soup
¼ cup water
2 stalks celery, chopped

In crock pot, place chops. In medium bowl, combine soup, water, and celery. Mix well. Pour over chops. Cover and cook on low 6 to 8 hours. ◆Makes 5 servings.

GRILL PORK ROAST

2 pounds pork loin roast
Salt
Pepper
1 (1 ounce) can whole cranberry sauce
1 (1 ounce) package dried onion soup

Season roast with salt and pepper. Place over indirect heat on grill. In medium bowl, combine cranberry sauce and onion soup. Mix well. Cover, microwave 1 minute. Baste roast with mixture, every 10 minutes for 45 to 50 minutes. ◆Makes 4 to 6 servings.

Apalachicola, **Florida,** was one of the busiest ports on the Gulf in the 19th century. Now it is a quaint little town of antebellum homes and historic houses. The Trinity Episcopal Church is the second oldest church in Florida with regularly scheduled services. It was prefabricated in New York of white pine. The sections traveled by schooner down the Atlantic Coast, around the Keys, and put together in Apalachicola.

FLAVOR PACKED PORK ROAST
▼ *(Crock pot)*

4 cups herb seasoned stuffing cubes
¾ cup chicken broth
½ cup chopped onions
2 to 2½ pounds boneless pork loin roast
½ cup apricot jam
1 tablespoon white vinegar

Coat inside crock pot with cooking spray. In medium bowl, combine stuffing, broth, and onions. Place in bottom of crock pot. Place roast on top of mixture. In small bowl, combine jam and vinegar. Mix well. brush mixture over roast. Cover and cook on low 7 to 8 hours. Stir stuffing before serving. ◆Makes 6 servings.

GLAZED COVER PORK LOIN
▼ *(Crock pot)*

1 (16 ounce) package baby carrots
4 boneless pork loin chops
1 (8 ounce) jar apricot preserves

In crock pot, place carrots. Top with pork. Brush pork with preserves. Cover and cook on high 4 hours, low 8 hours. ◆Makes 4 servings.

WASHINGTON TENDERLOINS

▼*(Crock pot)*

2 pounds pork loins
1 medium onion, sliced
2 apples, peeled, chopped
2 tablespoons apple jelly
1 tablespoon cider vinegar

In crock pot, combine all ingredients. Cover and cook on low 7 to 9 hours. Serve over rice. ◆Makes 4 servings.

NUTS ABOUT PORK

▼*(Crock pot)*

1 tablespoon soy sauce
1 tablespoon oil
4 garlic cloves, minced
¼ cup packed brown sugar
1½ pounds lean pork strips
½ cup cashews

In small bowl, combine soy sauce, oil, garlic, and brown sugar. Mix well. Place pork in crock pot. Top with mixture and add cashews. Cover and cook on low 5 to 6 hours, 2½ to 3 hours on high. ◆Makes 4 to 6 servings.

The nation's largest indoor and outdoor museum is Greenfield Village and Henry Ford Museum, a 260 acre complex with 100 historic buildings in **Dearborn, Michigan.** The museum is dedicated to the history of the automobile and its effect on the American way of life. The village includes Thomas Edison's laboratory, Henry Ford's birthplace and the Wright Brother's cycle shop.

Ashville, Ohio, displays the world's oldest traffic light every July 4th in their holiday celebration in Community Park. It is normally housed in the town's museum. It looks like an aluminum football with wings, and used a hypnoswirl process to change from red to green.

SPOUT ABOUT BBQ PORK
▼ *(Crock pot)*

2 to 3 pounds boneless pork loin
1 cup cola
¾ cup barbecue sauce
¼ cup ketchup

In crock pot, place pork. In small bowl, combine cola, sauce, and ketchup. Mix well. Pour mixture over pork. Cover and cook on high for 5 hours. ◆Makes 6 to 8 servings.

SHREDDED PORK FOR TACOS
▼ *(Crock pot)*

2 pounds boneless pork roast
1 (4 ounce) can chopped green chilies
½ teaspoon garlic salt
½ teaspoon pepper

In crock pot, combine all ingredients. Cover and cook on low 8 hours or until meat is tender. Use fork to shred pork. ◆Makes 6 servings.

HAM WITH COLA

▼ *(Crock pot)*

½ cup packed brown sugar
1 teaspoon cream horseradish
1 teaspoon dry mustard
⅓ cup cola soda
3 or 4 pound precooked ham

In small bowl, combine brown sugar, horseradish, mustard, and soda. Mix well. In crock pot, place ham. Brush mixture on top of ham. Cover and cook on low 6 hours, high 2 to 3 hours. ◆Makes 10 servings.

VIRGINIA GLAZED HAM

▼ *(Crock pot)*

5 pound ham
⅓ cup orange marmalade
1 tablespoon Dijon mustard
1 large oven roasting bag

In roasting bag, place ham. In small bowl, combine orange marmalade and mustard. Mix well. Spread mixture over ham. Seal bag and poke 4 holes in top of bag to vent. Place bag in crock pot and cook on low 6 to 8 hours. ◆Makes 8 servings.

At the center of **Indianapolis, Indiana,** is the "State Soldiers' and Sailors Monument." Monument Circle where it sets is the site of frequent festivals and lunchtime concerts. An elevator will take you up 230 feet to a glass-enclosed balcony, from which you can see the layout of the city. The 342-foot monument was dedicated in 1902 to Indiana war dead, in wars prior to World War I. It was designed, sculptured, executed and manufactured by Germans.

GOOD 'N TASTY HAM SKILLET

2 1 pound ham slices, fully cooked
½ cup water
⅓ cup honey mustard

Cut each ham slice into 4 serving pieces. In large skillet, combine water and honey mustard. Place ham in mixture, cover. Over medium heat bring to a boil. Reduce heat to low and simmer 15 minutes, turning ham once. ◆Makes 6 to 8 servings.

ON THE GRILL LAMB CHOPS

(Diabetic)

4 (5 ounce) lean lamb loin chops, 1 inch thick
½ cup frozen unsweetened apple juice, thawed
½ teaspoon ground cumin
½ teaspoon garlic powder
½ teaspoon curry powder

Trim fat from lamb. In medium bowl, combine apple juice, cumin, garlic, and curry. Place chops in mixture, coat both sides. Cover, refrigerate 6 hours. Coat grill rack with cooking spray. Place chops on grill. Cook 4 to 5 inches from heat. Grill 7 to 10 minutes on each side. ◆Makes 4 servings.

Per serving: *Exchange–3 lean meat, 1 starch; Calories–250; Carbohydrates–14.8 gm*

LEISURE DAY LAMB CHOPS

▼ *(Crock pot)*

2 tablespoons oil

6 lamb chops

½ cup orange juice

3 tablespoons honey

2 teaspoons salt

2 tablespoons cornstarch

1 teaspoon grated orange peel

In large skillet with oil, brown chops over medium heat. Drain. In small bowl, combine juice, honey, salt, cornstarch, and orange peel. Mix well. Brush lamb chops with mixture. In crock pot, place chops. Cover and cook on low 10 to 12 hours. ◆Makes 8 servings.

TASTY CHICKEN PARMESAN

4 boneless, skinless chicken breast

1 egg, beaten

¾ cup Italian seasoned dry bread crumbs

1 (26 ounce) jar pasta sauce

1 cup shredded mozzarella cheese

Preheat oven to 400 degrees. Dip chicken in egg, then in bread crumbs. Place chicken in 13x9 inch baking dish. Bake uncovered 20 minutes. Pour pasta sauce over chicken. Top with cheese and bake 15 minutes. ◆Makes 4 servings.

Automotive Art. Eight cars impaled on a spike are called "The Spindle," and a compact car flattened against a wall is "The Pinto Pelt." Dustin Shuler's creations are in the parking lot of the Cermak Plaza Shopping Center in **Berwyn, Illinois.**

STUFFING TOP CHICKEN

▼ *(Crock pot)*

6 boneless, skinless chicken breast

6 slices Swiss cheese

1 (10¾ ounce) can cream of
   mushroom soup

¼ cup milk

2 cups herb stuffing mix

½ cup butter, melted

Spray crock pot with cooking spray. Arrange chicken breast in crock pot. Top with cheese. In small bowl, combine soup and milk. Mix well. Spoon mixture over cheese. In a small bowl, combine stuffing mix and butter. Sprinkle stuffing on top. Cover and cook on low 8 to 10 hours, on high 4 to 6 hours. ◆Makes 6 servings.

SWEET AND SPICY CHICKEN

▼ *(Crock pot)*

1½ cups baby carrots, cut

2 pounds chicken breast, skinless

½ teaspoon red pepper

1½ cups sweet and sour sauce

1 (20 ounce) can pineapple chunks, drained

1 (16 ounce) package frozen bell pepper and onions,
   thawed and drained

In crock pot, place carrots, top with chicken, sprinkle with red pepper. Cover and cook on low 6 to 7 hours. Drain liquid from crock pot. Pour sweet and sour sauce over chicken. Add pineapple and bell pepper with onions. Cover and cook on high 60 minutes. Serve over rice. ◆Makes 6 servings.

SPUNKY BBQ CHICKEN

(Low fat/Low cal)

½ cup packed brown sugar

2 tablespoons oil

2 tablespoons cider vinegar

⅓ cup Grey Poupon® mustard

4 boneless, skinless chicken breast

In small bowl, combine brown sugar, oil, vinegar, and mustard. Mix well. Baste chicken breasts with mixture. Grill 4 to 6 inches from heat, 15 to 20 minutes. Baste chicken often when grilling. ◆Makes 4 servings

Per serving: *Calories–303; Protein–27 gm; Fat–12 gm; Carbohydrates–2 gm; Cholesterol–66 mg; Sodium–402 mg*

FAMILY PLEASING BBQ CHICKEN

(Low fat/Low cal)

⅓ cup apple jelly

1 tablespoon honey

1 tablespoon Dijon mustard

½ teaspoon cinnamon

½ teaspoon salt

4 boneless, skinless chicken breast

In small bowl, combine jelly, honey, mustard, cinnamon, and salt. Mix well. Brush chicken breast with mixture. Cook on grill 4 to 6 inches from heat. Grill 15 to 20 minutes ◆Makes 4 servings.

Per serving: *Calories–160; Protein–27 gm; Fat–5 gm; Carbohydrates–6 gm; Cholesterol–73 gm; Sodium–160 gm*

Galena, Illinois, produced more generals in the Civil War than any other town. Why not? It was the hometown of General Ulysses S. Grant, later president of the U.S. His 1860 Italianate home, with original furnishings and personal items, is a Historic Site. The Galena post office (1857-59) is the second oldest continuously operating post office in the country.

TIME FOR A PICNIC FRIED CHICKEN

1½ teaspoon salt

1 teaspoon pepper

2½ to 3 pounds chicken, cut up

1 cup flour

½ cup oil

Salt and pepper chicken, dredge in flour. In large skillet, heat oil over medium high heat until hot. Place chicken in skillet, brown on all sides. Reduce heat to low. Cover and cook 20 minutes. Uncover, turn heat to high, cook 5 minutes longer turning frequently. ◆Makes 4 to 6 servings.

CREAMY GARLIC CHICKEN

1 tablespoon oil

4 boneless chicken breast halves

1 (10¾ ounce) can cream of garlic soup

½ cup milk

In large skillet with oil, heat over medium heat until hot. Add chicken and brown on all sides. Add soup and milk. Cover, reduce heat to low and simmer 10 minutes. ◆Makes 4 servings.

EASY CRISPY CHICKEN

1 (10¾ ounce) can cream of chicken soup
½ cup milk
1 (1 ounce) envelope ranch salad dressing
4 chicken breast, skinless
1½ cups finely crushed tortilla chips
2 tablespoons butter or margarine

Preheat oven to 400 degrees. In medium bowl, combine soup, milk, and salad dressing. Mix well. Dip chicken into mixture. Coat with tortilla chips. Place chicken on greased baking sheet. Drizzle butter over chicken. Bake 30 minutes or until chicken is no longer pink. ◆Makes 4 servings.

SAUCE GLAZED CHICKEN

(Low fat/Low cal)

½ cup apricot preserves
1 tablespoon chili sauce
½ teaspoon salt
2 teaspoons Dijon mustard
4 large skinless chicken breast

Preheat oven to 425 degrees. In small bowl, combine apricots, chili sauce, salt, and mustard. Mix well. Arrange chicken in 13x9 inch baking dish. Brush with apricot glaze. Bake 30 minutes, brushing occasionally with glaze. ◆Makes 4 servings.

Per serving: *Calories–338; Protein–43 gm; Fat–2 gm; Carbohydrates–35 gm; Cholesterol–107 gm; Sodium–548 mg*

CHEESY CHICKEN TENDERS

4 boneless, skinless chicken breast halves

1 cup crushed cheese flavored crackers

½ cup shredded cheddar cheese

2 eggs

Preheat oven to 400 degrees. Coat 15½x10½x1 inch baking pan with cooking spray. Cut chicken into ½ inch strips. In medium bowl, combine crackers and cheese. In large bowl, beat eggs. Add chicken strips. Coat well. Dip chicken in cracker mixture, toss to coat. Place coated chicken in pan. Bake 12 to 15 minutes. ◆Makes 4 servings.

COCK OF THE WALK DRUMSTICKS

(Diabetic)

1 teaspoon chili powder

¼ teaspoon garlic powder

¼ teaspoon ground thyme

¼ teaspoon oregano

8 (about 1½ pounds) chicken drum sticks, skinned

Olive oil flavored vegetable cooking spray

1 cup crushed low fat barbecue potato chips

Preheat oven to 350 degrees. In small bowl, combine chili, garlic, thyme, and oregano. Mix well. Coat drumsticks with cooking spray. Sprinkle mixture evenly over drumsticks. Place on plate, cover and chill 30 minutes. Dredge drumsticks in crushed chips. Place drumsticks on a rack in a roasting pan. Bake 20 minutes. Turn drumsticks, bake 15 minutes. ◆Makes 4 servings.

Per serving: *Exchanges–3 very lean meat, 1 starch, 1 fat; Calories– 198; Carbohydrates–12.1 gm*

TURKEY ANYTIME

▼ *(Crock pot)*

4 to 6 pound turkey breast

1 (15 ounce) can whole cranberry sauce

½ cup orange juice

½ teaspoon salt

1 (1 ounce) envelope dry onion soup

In crock pot, place turkey. In medium bowl, combine cranberry sauce, orange juice, salt, and onion soup mix. Mix well. Pour over turkey. Cover and cook on low 8 hours. ◆Makes 6 to 8 servings.

The Be Good to Your Mother-In-Law Bridge was built in 1905 in **Croswell, Minnesota,** and has been rebuilt three times. A sign at one end of the bridge advises couples to be good to their mother's-in-law, and at the other end a sign advises them to love one another. It is a ritual for couples to be photographed under the sign, then walk hand-in-hand across the 139 foot bridge.

Howl at the wolves. About half the time they will howl back at you in a **Minnesota** North Woods night in Ely. At the International Wolf Center you can learn much about these much-maligned creatures and participate in an evening Wolf Howl.

GRILLED TURKEY BURGERS

1½ pounds ground turkey
¼ cup Miracle Whip®
4 ounces crumbled blue cheese

In medium bowl, combine all ingredients. Mix well. Shape mixture into 6 patties. Grill patties 4 to 5 inches from heat 15 to 20 minutes. Serve on buns. ◆Makes 6 servings.

ARKANSAS POLE CATFISH

¾ cup yellow cornmeal
¼ cup flour
2 teaspoons pepper
cooking oil
6 catfish fillets

In large shallow dish, combine cornmeal, flour, salt, and pepper. In deep cast iron skillet, pour oil to a depth of 1½ inches, heat over medium heat until hot. Dredge fish in mixture and place in skillet. Fry in batches on both sides until golden brown 5 to 7 minutes. ◆Makes 6 servings.

CRUSTY FRIED CATFISH

¾ cup cornmeal

2 tablespoons flour

½ teaspoon salt

½ cup milk

6 catfish fillets

oil

In medium bowl, combine cornmeal, flour, and salt. Mix well. Dip catfish fillets, one at a time, into milk then into cornmeal mixture. Set fillets aside for 10 minutes to set the crust. In a large skillet, heat oil over medium heat until hot. Add catfish and cook until a deep golden brown. ◆Makes 6 servings.

MINNESOTA ALMOND WALLEYE

4 walleye fillets

4 teaspoons butter or margarine, melted

4 teaspoons lemon juice

½ teaspoon red pepper

½ cup slivered almonds

Place fillets in a single layer in a broiler pan. Cover fillets with butter and lemon juice. Sprinkle red pepper over fillets. Cover fillets with almonds. Broil 10 to 15 minutes or until tops of fillets are browned and pull apart with fork. Can be grilled. ◆Makes 4 servings.

The ultimate in outhouses may be the two-story, five hole comfort station at the 1871 Hooper-Bowler-Hillstrom house in **Belle Plain, Minnesota.** It has a skyway connecting it to the main house. The upper seat is placed further back than the lower level so materials can safely fall behind the wall.

ON THE BARBIE GRILLED TROUT

2 pan dressed, 1 pound trout
½ teaspoon salt
1 orange, sliced
1 small onion, sliced

Spray 2 large sheets of heavy foil with cooking spray. Place one trout on each sheet. Sprinkle each trout with salt. Fill each with orange slices, cover with onions. Fold the edges of each foil square together to make a packet. Place on grill over medium heat. Cook 25 minutes turn once. ◆Makes 2 servings.

TINA'S OKLAHOMA PRIDE STRIPER

2 eggs
¼ cup milk
1 teaspoon salt
½ teaspoon pepper
4 (1 pound each) striper fillets
1 cup bread crumbs
½ cup oil

In medium bowl, combine eggs, milk, salt, and pepper. Mix well. Dip fillets in egg mixture then in bread crumbs. In large skillet, heat oil over medium heat until hot. Place fillets in skillet, cook 8 to 10 minutes, brown both sides. ◆Makes 4 servings.

GRILLED STYLE HALIBUT

(Low fat/Low cal)

2 tablespoons lemon juice

3 tablespoons olive oil

2 garlic cloves, diced

1 teaspoon oregano

½ teaspoon salt

4 (6 ounce) halibut steaks, ¾ inch thick

In medium bowl, combine lemon juice, oil, garlic, oregano, and salt. Mix well. Place fillets in mixture. Cover and chill one hour. Grill halibut over high heat. Brushing with mixture during grilling, grill 3 to 4 minutes per side. ◆Makes 4 servings.

Per serving: *Calories–199; Protein–29 gm; Fat–8 gm; Carbohydrates–1 gm; Cholesterol–44 mg; Sodium–218 mg*

GRILL THAT TUNA

3 pounds tuna, cut into serving size

¾ cup prepared ranch salad dressing

Place tuna on heavy foil, cover tuna with salad dressing. Seal foil, place on grill over medium heat 20 to 30 minutes, or until tuna flakes when tested with a fork. Also great for catfish. ◆Makes 6 servings.

Since 1936 nearly six billion cans of Spam have been produced and sold around the world by Hormel Foods. Now at the 16,500 square foot Spam Museum in **Austin, Minnesota,** you can see a display showing the role Spam played in World War II, participate in a simulated Spam production line and play an interactive game based on Spam trivia.

Star Trek fans can visit the birthplace of Capt. James T. Kirk and attend his birthday celebration the last Saturday in June at **Riverside, Iowa.** His birth site on March 21, 2228, is marked behind a barber shop. You can buy vials of Kirk Dirt and see a model of the "USS Riverside" in the town square.

SWORDFISH AND SALSA

(Diabetic)

6 (4 ounce) swordfish steaks, ¾ inch thick

⅓ cup lime juice

⅓ cup beer

1½ tablespoons vegetable oil

1 tablespoon ground cumin

1 tablespoon Dijon mustard

¼ teaspoon salt

2 cloves garlic, diced

In medium bowl, place steaks. In small bowl, combine lime juice, beer, oil, cumin, mustard, salt, and garlic. Mix well. Pour mixture over steaks. Cover, marinate 30 minutes. Place steaks on grill. Cook 4 to 5 inches form heat. Cool 4 to 6 minutes on each side. Serve with salsa recipe below. ◆Makes 6 servings.

Per serving: *Exchanges–3 lean meat, 1 vegetable; Calories–179; Carbohydrates–6.1 gm*

Salsa

1 cup diced tomato

⅓ cup diced onion

¼ cup diced green pepper

1½ tablespoon lime juice

4 teaspoons dried cilantro

1 teaspoon diced jalapeno pepper

1 clove garlic, minced

¼ cup no salt added tomato juice

¼ teaspoon salt

⅛ teaspoon ground cumin

In medium cowl, combine all ingredients. Cover, chill 40 minutes. Serve with swordfish.

ALASKA GRILLED SALMON

4 tablespoons fresh lemon juice

2 tablespoons packed brown sugar

2 tablespoons soy sauce

6 (6 ounce) salmon steaks or fillets

In small bowl, combine lemon juice, sugar, and soy sauce. Mix well. Brush mixture over salmon. Grill 5 to 6 inches from heat. Grill 10 to 12 minutes. ◆Makes 6 servings.

Holland amid the cornfields. **Pella, Iowa,** even has a McDonalds with a Dutch look. The Klokkenspel, a musical clock sets animated figures in motion that tell of Pella's history. A computer-driven 147 bell carillon provides music. It is only one of two or three animated clock towers in the U.S. Thousands of tulips are especially colorful during the annual Tulip Time, the second weekend in May.

OREGON SALMON CAKES

1 (12 ounce) can pink salmon, drained
⅓ cup diced onions
1 egg, beaten
½ cup flour
1½ teaspoon baking powder
½ cup oil

In medium bowl, flake salmon with a fork. Add onions and egg. Mix well. In small bowl, combine flour and baking powder, gradually add to salmon mixture. Mix well. Divide mixture into 6 balls. Pat balls into patties. In large skillet with oil, heat over medium heat until hot. Place patties in skillet. Cook 10 minutes or until golden brown. ◆Makes 6 servings.

NEW ORLEAN'S SAUTÉED SHRIMP

(Low fat/Low cal)

1 pound large fresh shrimp, peeled and deveined
3 tablespoons margarine or butter
1 clove garlic, diced
¼ cup dry white wine

In large skillet, combine shrimp, butter, and garlic. Over medium heat, cook 5 minutes. Add wine, cook 2 to 3 minutes. ◆Makes 4 servings.

Per serving: *Calories–165; Protein–14 gm; Fat–9 gm; Carbohydrates–1 gm; Cholesterol–131 mg*

MAINE STEAMED LOBSTER

2 (1½ pounds each) live lobsters
4 tablespoons butter, melted
2 teaspoons fresh lemon juice

In large pot, heat 1½ inches water to boiling over high heat. Plunge lobsters head first, into boiling water. Cover and heat to boiling. Steam 13 minutes. With tongs, transfer lobsters to colander to drain, then place on platter. Combine butter and lemon juice. Pour into small cups for dipping lobster. ◆Makes 2 servings.

HORSERADISH SAUCE FOR BEEF

½ cup sour cream
1 tablespoon cream style horseradish
1 teaspoon mayonnaise

In small bowl, combine all ingredients. Mix well. Serve with beef. ◆Makes ½ cup.

Herbert Hoover, who was President of the United States during the Depression, was born in a modest cottage in the small settlement of **West Branch, Iowa,** in 1874. He was of Quaker ancestry, and was the first U.S. President born west of the Mississippi River. His birthplace and the Herbert Hoover Museum and Presidential Library are located just east of Iowa City.

Think the "Duke" was a true cowboy from the Wild West? Wrong. He grew up among the cornfields of south central **Iowa** in the little town of Winterset. Marion Morrison's modest boyhood home is restored as it was in 1907 and is open to the public. He played football in California and became one of Hollywood's most rugged stars, especially in western movies, John Wayne.

DIPPING SAUCE FOR BARBECUE

1 cup ketchup
½ cup chili sauce
½ cup packed brown sugar
2 tablespoons cider vinegar
1 tablespoon lemon juice
1 tablespoon liquid smoke

In 2 quart saucepan, combine all ingredients. Bring to a boil over medium heat. Reduce heat to low, simmer uncovered 10 minutes, stirring occasionally. Serve with grilled chicken. ◆Makes 2 cups.

GRILLING BBQ SAUCE

½ cup ketchup
¼ cup water
3 tablespoons brown sugar
1 teaspoon sugar
¼ teaspoon liquid smoke

In small saucepan, combine all ingredients. Over low heat, simmer 15 minutes. Brush meat with sauce before grilling.

DON'T PASS UP HOT DOG SAUCE

(Crock pot)

2 pounds ground beef

1½ cups chopped onion

1 (12 ounce) can beer

2½ tablespoons chili powder

1 (15 ounce) can tomato sauce

2 cups ketchup

¼ cup mustard

In medium skillet, brown beef over medium heat. Drain. Add beer and chili powder, reduce heat to low simmer 10 minutes. Add tomato sauce, ketchup, and mustard. Mix well. Pour mixture in crock pot. Cover and cook on low 2½ to 3 hours. ◆Makes 6 to 8 servings.

CHILI CHICKEN OR PORK RUB

1 tablespoon chili powder

1 teaspoon ground cumin

¼ teaspoon red pepper

¼ teaspoon salt

1 large clove garlic, diced

In small bowl, combine all ingredients. Mix well. Rub evenly on both sides of chicken or chops before grilling. ◆Makes ½ cup.

The final section of the Gateway Arch in **St. Louis, Missouri,** had to be put in place at sunrise–before the heat expanded the arch and kept it from fitting. The 630 feet stainless steel arch commemorates St. Louis' role as Gateway to the West.

MARINADE FOR GRILLING CHICKEN

½ cup soy sauce
½ cup orange juice
2 tablespoons sugar
2 tablespoons vegetable oil
2 teaspoons ground ginger
2 cloves garlic, crushed

In medium bowl, combine all ingredients. Add chicken, turn to coat. Chill 1 hour before grilling. ◆Makes 1 cup.

TARTAR SAUCE FOR FISH

1 cup mayonnaise
½ cup sweet pickle relish, drained
2½ teaspoons lemon juice

In small bowl, combine all ingredients. Mix well. Chill until ready to serve. ◆Makes 1½ cups.

SHRIMP COCKTAIL SAUCE

½ cup ketchup
3 tablespoons creamy horseradish
¼ teaspoon Tabasco® sauce
1 tablespoon lemon juice
1 teaspoon sugar
1 teaspoon Worcestershire sauce

In small bowl, combine all ingredients. Cover and chill. ◆Makes ¾ cup.

Tin Can Lizzie

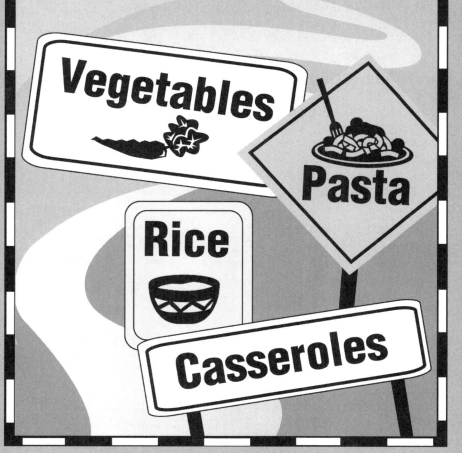

TIME ZONES

The fifty United States are in six time zones: Eastern, Central, Mountain, Pacific, Alaskan, and Aleutian-Hawaiian. Arizona, Hawaii and parts of Indiana do not observe Daylight Savings Time.

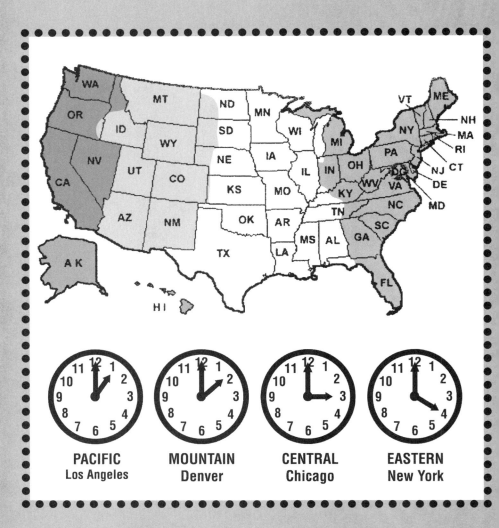

PACIFIC
Los Angeles

MOUNTAIN
Denver

CENTRAL
Chicago

EASTERN
New York

GRILLED ASPARAGUS

(Diabetic)

½ pound fresh asparagus

2 teaspoons reduced calorie margarine

¼ teaspoon lemon pepper seasoning

Clean and snap off tough ends of asparagus. Remove scales. Cut a large square of heavy duty aluminum foil. Place asparagus in the middle of foil. Spread margarine over asparagus. Sprinkle pepper over top. Fold aluminum foil tightly to seal. Place on grill and cook over medium heat 10 minutes. ◆Makes 2 servings.

Per serving: *Exchange–1 vegetable, ½ fat; Calories–35; Carbohydrates–2.9 gm*

LICKETY SPLIT CHEESE BROCCOLI

■*(Microwave)*

1 (10¾ ounce) can cheddar cheese soup

¼ cup milk

4 cups frozen broccoli cuts

In 2 quart casserole, combine all ingredients. Mix well. Cover and microwave on high 8 minutes or until broccoli is tender crisp. Stir once during cooking. ◆Makes 4 servings.

You can actually dig for diamonds (and keep what you find) at Crater of Diamonds State Park near **Murfreesboro, Arkansas.** Almost 1,000 diamonds are found every year. The largest was found in 1924 and weighed 40.35 carats. In 1975 a 16.37 carat diamond was found. Arkansas is the only state to produce both pearls and diamonds.

CROCK POT CANDIED CARROTS

▼ *(Crock Pot)*

4 (16 ounce) packages frozen sliced carrots
1 (12 ounce) bottle maple syrup
½ cup brown sugar, packed

In crock pot, combine all ingredients. Mix well. Cover and cook on high 6 hours. ◆Makes 15 to 20 servings.

CABBAGE AND APPLES SWEET DISH

(Diabetic)

2 teaspoons butter
1 medium onion, chopped
1 small head red cabbage, chopped
1 apple, peeled and thinly sliced
¼ cup apple juice
¾ cup water
1 tablespoon red wine vinegar

In large skillet, melt butter over low heat. Add onions, cook 1 minute. Add cabbage and apples, cook 5 minutes. In small bowl, combine apple juice, water, and vinegar. Pour over cabbage mixture. Cover and cook on low heat for 30 minutes. ◆Makes 4 servings.

Per serving: *Exchanges–1 vegetable, ½ fruit, ½ fat; Calories–87; Carbohydrates–16 gm*

I'LL BRING THE CAULIFLOWER

▼ *(Crock pot, Low fat/ Low cal)*

8 cups cauliflower florets

1 large onion, thinly sliced

1 (16 ounce) jar cheddar cheese pasta sauce

½ teaspoon pepper

In crock pot, combine all ingredients. Mix well. Cover and cook on high 3 hours, low 6 hours. ◆Makes 10 to 12 servings.

Per serving: *Calories–59; Protein–3 gm; Fat–6 gm; Carbohydrate–8 gm; Sodium–329 mg*

OHIO'S CORN BAKE

1 (14 ounce) can cream style corn, undrained

1 (14 ounce) can whole kernel corn, undrained

½ cup butter, melted

1 cup sour cream

2 eggs

1 box Jiffy® cornbread mix

Preheat oven to 350 degrees. In large bowl, combine all ingredients. Mix well. Pour into 9x13 inch baking dish. Bake 50 to 60 minutes. ◆Makes 6 to 8 servings.

Near **Eureka Springs, Arkansas,** is the unique Thorncrown Chapel. The unusual architecture has a local sandstone base, cross-braced hand rubbed 2 by 4 and 2 by 6 timbers, more than 6,000 square feet of glass in the walls and central skylight that let the chapel blend into the surrounding forest as it were grown there. It is 60 feet long, 24 feet tall and holds about 100 people.

SUPER TASTY CORN ON THE COB

(Diabetic)

1 tablespoon dillweed

1 tablespoon thyme

1 tablespoon water

1 tablespoon vegetable oil

1 clove garlic, minced

4 medium ears corn

Preheat oven to 450 degrees. In small bowl, combine dillweed, thyme, water, oil, and garlic. Mix well. Spread over corn. Place each ear on a piece of heavy duty aluminum foil, wrap lightly. Grill or bake at 450 degrees for 25 minutes. ◆Makes 4 servings.

Per Serving: *Exchanges–1 starch, 1 fat; Calories–106; Carbohydrates–18.1 gm*

SAUCY CORN AND BROCCOLI

▼*(Crock pot, Low fat/Low cal)*

1 (16 ounce) package frozen cut broccoli

1 (16 ounce) package frozen corn

1(10¾ ounce) can cream of chicken soup

1½ cups shredded American cheese

¼ cup milk

In crock pot, coat with cooking spray. Combine all ingredients in crock pot. Mix well. Cover and cook on high 2½ hours on low 5 hours. ◆Makes 8 to 10 servings.

Per Serving: *Calories–191; Protein–9 gr; Fat–10 gr; Carbohydrates–19 gr; Sodium–548 mg*

ARKANSAS FRIED OKRA

2 eggs
12 ounces okra, cut into 1 inch
  pieces
½ cup corn meal
½ teaspoon salt
oil

In medium bowl, beat eggs. Add okra
and toss to coat. In small bowl, combine corn meal and salt. Add okra and
toss to coat. In medium skillet heat
¼ inch oil over medium heat until hot.
Fry okra in small batches 2 to 3 minutes or until golden. Drain on paper
towels. ◆Makes 4 servings.

FRIED GREEN TOMATOES

2 eggs, beaten
4 medium green tomatoes, sliced
1 cup corn meal
oil

In medium bowl, add eggs. Dip tomatoes in eggs. In small bowl, add corn
meal. Dip tomatoes in corn meal, coat
well. In large skillet with oil, heat
until hot over medium high heat. Add
tomatoes, brown on both sides until
golden brown. ◆Makes 6 servings.

In downtown
**Eureka Springs,
Arkansas,** no
streets intersect
at a right angle.
The picturesque
Victorian town is
built on the hill-
sides of the
beautiful Ozarks.
It became a tour-
ist attraction
originally for its
many springs
and bathhouses.
It has been
revived as an
entertainment
and shopping
area. A church
entered through
its bell tower
and the "Great
Passion Play"
each summer
are some of the
attractions.

VEGGIES WITH A SPIN

(Diabetic)

¾ cup chopped tomatoes
¼ cup chopped green pepper
¼ cup chopped green onion
1½ cups frozen egg substitute, thawed
¼ cup skim milk
¼ cup shredded cheddar cheese
⅛ teaspoon pepper
⅛ teaspoon hot sauce

In large nonstick skillet, coat with cooking spray. Combine tomatoes, green pepper, and green onions. Cook over medium heat 5 minutes. In large bowl combine egg substitute, milk, cheese, pepper, and hot sauce. Pour over skillet mixture and continue cooking over medium heat until mixture is firm. Serve immediately. ◆Makes 6 servings.

Per serving: *Exchanges–1½ lean meat; Calories–92; Carbohydrates–3.2 gm*

ALABAMA SOUTHERN GRITS

4 cups water
1 teaspoon salt
1 cup grits
1 tablespoon butter

In large saucepan, add water and salt over medium heat, bring to a boil. Add grits slowly, stirring often. Add butter. Reduce heat to low. Cover and cook 30 to 40 minutes. Makes 4 servings.

SHORTCUT STROMBOLI LOG

1 (10 ounce) refrigerate pizza dough

1 (10¾ ounce) can cream of celery soup

1 cup cooked broccoli

2 cups cooked ham

1 cup shredded cheddar cheese

Preheat oven to 400 degrees. Unroll dough onto greased baking sheet, set aside. In medium bowl, combine soup, broccoli, and ham. Spread mixture down center of dough. Top with cheese. Fold long side of dough over filling, pinch to seal. Bake for 20 minutes or until brown. ◆Makes 4 servings.

MARYLAND FETTUCCINE

1 (12 ounce) package fettuccine noodles, cooked, drained

¾ cup grated Parmesan cheese

¾ cup half and half

3 tablespoons butter or margarine

2 tablespoons parsley

¼ teaspoon pepper

In large saucepan, combine all ingredients. Cook over medium heat until hot. ◆Makes 4 servings.

Ft. Smith, Arkansas, was established in 1817 to help keep peace among the area's Indians. It is most famous for the court of Hanging Judge Isaac Parker. With very few underpaid deputy marshals, he was to provide law and order for the whole of Indian Territory. Justice was swift and sure. Judge Parker sentenced about 140 people to hang, and 68 did die on his gallows. The restored courthouse and gallows are open to the public.

Memorial Day is said to have originated in **Columbus, Mississippi.** The town's Friendship Cemetery is called the place "Where Flowers Healed a Nation." A year after the Civil War ended, on April 25, 1866, some of the town women decorated both the Confederate and Union solder's graves with flowers. This started a tradition that soon became known as Decoration Day.

WISCONSIN CHEESE PASTA BAKE

4 cups cooked corkscrew pasta

1 (10¾ ounce) can cream of mushroom soup

1 (8 ounce) package shredded two cheese blend

½ cup grated Parmesan cheese

1 cup milk

Preheat oven to 400 degrees. In 1½ quart casserole, combine all ingredients. Bake for 30 minutes. ◆Makes 4 servings.

OLD RELIABLE BEEF PIZZA

¾ pound ground beef

1 cup chopped green pepper

½ cup chopped onion

1 (10 ounce) pre baked thin crust Italian pizza crust

1 (8 ounce) can pizza sauce

1½ cup shredded mozzarella cheese

Preheat oven to 425 degrees. In medium skillet, brown beef, bell pepper, and onion over medium heat. Drain grease. Place pizza crust on ungreased cookie sheet. Spread pizza sauce over crust. Top with beef mixture and cheese. Bake for 10 to 12 minutes or until cheese is melted. ◆Makes 6 servings.

NO FUSS RAVIOLI

1 (9 ounce) package refrigerated chicken ravioli
1 tablespoon butter
1 cup ranch dressing
½ cup grated Parmesan cheese

In medium saucepan, cook ravioli according to package, drain. In large nonstick skillet, combine all ingredients. Cook over medium heat until hot. Sprinkle cheese over mixture. Makes 3 to 4 servings.

WAGON WHEEL PASTA SKILLET

1 pound lean ground beef, cooked and drained
1 cup water
⅓ cup barbecue sauce
1 (16 ounce) can baked beans, undrained
1 (8 ounce) can tomato sauce
1¼ cup uncooked wagon wheel pasta

In large skillet, combine beef, water, barbecue sauce, baked beans, and tomato sauce. Bring to a boil. Add pasta. Reduce heat. Cover and simmer 10 to 15 minutes or until pasta is tender. Makes 4 servings.

The Blues Archive at the **University of Mississippi** in Oxford has the world's largest collection of blues recordings. The Blues are a musical style native to the United States, and traces its beginnings to the Mississippi Delta cotton fields.

The smallest church in the world is the Madonna Church of Bayou Goula, **Louisiana**. It has only room for three people- about six square feet in area.

NEBRASKA BEEF AND MAC SKILLET

1 pound ground beef

1 small onion, chopped

1 (10¾ ounce) can tomato soup

¼ cup water

1 tablespoon Worcestershire sauce

¾ cup shredded cheese

2 cups cooked macaroni

In medium skillet, brown beef and onion over medium heat. Drain grease. Add soup, water, Worcestershire sauce, cheese and macaroni. Reduce heat to low. Simmer 10 minutes. ◆Makes 4 servings.

OUT ALL DAY BEEF STOGANOFF

▼(Crock pot)

4 pounds stewing beef, cut into 1 inch cubes

1 (10¾ ounce) cream of mushroom soup

2 (1 ounce) packages onion soup mix

1 (8 ounce) container sour cream

In crock pot, combine all ingredients. Cover and cook on low 8 hours. Serve over noodles. ◆Makes 6 to 8 servings.

POTATOES AND SAUSAGE CASSEROLE

▼ *(Crock pot)*

8 to 10 large potatoes, peeled, sliced
1 pound sausage links
2½ cups shredded cheese
1 (10¾ ounce) can cream of
  mushroom soup
1 cup milk
1 teaspoon salt

In crock pot, combine all ingredients, mix well. Cover and cook on low 6 to 8 hours. ◆Makes 8 to 10 servings.

PIZZA TASTING CASSEROLE

▼ *(Crock pot)*

1 pound ground beef, browned,
  drained
1 small onion, chopped
2 (15 ounce) cans pizza sauce
1 (8 ounce) package pepperoni sliced
1 cup macaroni, cooked, drained

In crock pot, combine all ingredients. Mix well. Cover and cook on low 3 hours. ◆Makes 6 servings.

Write a hit song and become governor. Jimmie Davis co-wrote "You Are My Sunshine" in 1940. He was elected governor of **Louisiana.** He also wrote other songs and is in the Country Music Hall of Fame.

The Enchanted Highway, a 32 mile road between Regent and Gladstone, **North Dakota,** has some spectacular giant metal folk art sculpture. You can see a flock of 60 foot pheasants, a giant grasshopper and Teddy Roosevelt riding a horse.

IN MINUTES RICE DISH

1 (10½ ounce) can chicken broth

¾ cup water

1 tablespoon butter

2 cup uncooked Minute Rice®

In medium saucepan, combine chicken broth, water, and butter. Over medium heat bring to a boil. Stir in rice. Cover and remove from heat. Let stand 5 minutes. Fluff with fork. ◆Makes 4 servings.

RICE LOVER'S FRIED RICE

2 eggs

2 tablespoons water

2 tablespoons vegetable oil

3 green onions, chopped with tops

3 cups cold cooked rice

⅓ pound cooked shrimp, chopped

3 tablespoons soy sauce

In small bowl, beat eggs and water, set aside. In a large skillet, heat oil over medium heat. Add green onions. Cook 30 seconds. Add eggs and scramble. Stir in rice and cook until hot, gently separating grains. Add shrimp and soy sauce. Cook and stir until heated through. ◆Makes 6 servings.

ON THE CAPE
RICE AND SHRIMP

2 boil in the bag rice

1 (12 ounce) jar Alfredo sauce

1 (10 ounce) can diced tomatoes
  with basil

1 pound grilled shrimp

½ cup shredded Parmesan cheese

Prepare rice according to package directions. In medium saucepan combine Alfredo sauce and tomatoes. Heat over low heat. Add shrimp. Pour mixture over rice. Top with cheese. ◆Makes 6 servings.

SPAM-TAS-TIC
CAMP CASSEROLE

2 (12 ounce) cans Spam®, cubed

1 medium onion, chopped

1 teaspoon butter

3 (15 ounce) cans green beans,
  drained

3 (8 ounce) cans tomato sauce

1 teaspoon garlic powder

½ teaspoon salt

In large skillet, brown Spam and onions in butter. Add green beans, tomato sauce, garlic powder, and salt. Mix well. Cover and simmer 30 minutes. Can cook over an open fire. Serve over rice. ◆Makes 6 to 8 servings.

No one driving I-90 in **South Dakota** can resist the lure of hundreds of billboards advertising the Wall Drug Store. It started in 1931 with road signs advertising free ice water to hot, thirsty travelers. The western-themed complex now has shops, restaurants, museums and entertainment that draws up to 20,000 visitors daily in the summer.

Work continues on the world's largest sculpture in the **Black Hills of South Dakota.** All four presidents carved in Mt. Rushmore would fit into the head of the Crazy Horse Monument. Since it was begun in 1948 over eight million tons of granite have been blasted away. When completed the sculpture of Crazy Horse on his stallion will be 641 feet long and 563 feet high.

CHILI AND TAMALE CASSEROLE

2 (14 ounce) cans chili con carne
6 tamales
½ cup chopped onions
2 cups corn chips
1 cup grated cheddar cheese

Preheat oven to 350 degrees. In 2 quart casserole, cover bottom with chili. Add tamales, onions, chips, and cheese. Bake for 30 minutes. ◆Makes 4 to 6 servings.

NEW JERSEY SAUSAGE CASSEROLE

1 (28 ounce) package frozen chunky style hash browns, thawed
1 (14 ounce) can sauerkraut, drained, rinsed
1 (10¾ ounce) can cream of mushroom soup
1⅓ cups half and half
1 (16 ounce) package polish sausage, sliced

Preheat oven to 375 degrees. In large bowl, combine all ingredients. Mix well. Coat a 13x9 inch baking dish with cooking spay. Pour mixture in dish. Bake 50 minutes. ◆Makes 6 servings.

ONE FOR ALL CHICKEN DINNER

▼ *(Crock pot)*

3 pounds whole chicken, cut up

4 carrots, peeled and sliced

4 potatoes, peeled and sliced

2 celery stalks, sliced

1 cup Italian dressing

½ cup chicken broth

In crock pot, place chicken. Add carrots, potatoes, celery, and onions. Pour dressing and broth over vegetables. Cover and cook on low 6 to 8 hours. ◆Makes 6 servings.

ONE DISH CHICKEN CASSEROLE

1 (10¾ ounce) can cream of mushroom soup

1 cup water

¾ cup uncooked white rice

½ teaspoon paprika

4 skinless, boneless chicken halves

Preheat oven to 375 degrees. In 2 quart baking dish, combine soup, water, rice, and paprika. Place chicken on mixture. Cover and bake 50 minutes or until chicken is no longer pink. ◆Makes 4 servings.

The Great Platte River Road Archway Monument near **Kearney, Nebraska,** spans Interstate 80. Exhibits commemorate the region's historical importance to western navigation and travel. The Platte River was the primary westward route for the Oregon, California and Mormon Trails.

PLAY 'N EAT CHICKEN DINNER

▼ *(Crock pot)*

4 skinless, boneless, chicken breasts

1 (10¾ ounce) can cream of chicken soup

⅓ cup milk

1 (6 ounce) package stuffing mix

1⅔ cup hot water

In crock pot, place chicken. In small bowl, combine soup and milk. Mix well. Pour mixture over chicken. In medium bowl, combine stuffing mix and water. Spoon stuffing over chicken. Cover and cook on low 6 to 8 hours. ◆Makes 4 servings.

CHICKEN POT PIE

1 (10¾ ounce) can cream of chicken soup

1 cup chopped cooked chicken

1 (16 ounce) package frozen vegetables

1¼ cup Bisquick®

½ cup milk

1 egg

Preheat oven to 400 degrees. In 9 inch pie pan, combine soup, chicken, and vegetables. In medium bowl, combine Bisquick®, milk, and egg. Mix well. Pour over chicken mixture. Bake 30 minutes. ◆Makes 4 servings.

OUTING DAY SUPPER

▼ *(Crock pot)*

2 pounds ground beef, browned, drained

3 ribs celery, chopped

½ green pepper, chopped

1 small onion, chopped

1 teaspoon sugar

½ teaspoon salt

1 (10¾ ounce) can cream of mushroom soup

In crock pot, combine all ingredients. Cover and cook on low 8 to 10 hours. Serve over biscuits or with cheddar cheese. ◆Makes 6 to 8 servings.

JUST AHEAD POTATOES AND BEEF

(Low cal/Low fat)

1 (17 ounce) package fully cooked beef tips with gravy

2 cups frozen chunky style hash brown potatoes

1 red bell pepper, cut in 1 inch strips

1 green bell pepper, cut in 1 inch strips

1 small onion, cut in wedges

½ cup water

In large skillet, combine all ingredients. Over medium heat, bring to a boil. Stir occasionally. Reduce heat. Cover and simmer 15 minutes. ◆Makes 4 servings.

Per serving: *Calories–247; Protein–21 gm; Fat–6 gm; Carbohydrates–28 gm; Cholesterol–46 mg; Sodium–600 mg*

Carhenge, near **Alliance, Nebraska**, is a replica of Stonehenge, using 33 cars instead of stones. It violated land use laws and was scheduled for removal. Friends came to its rescue and it is now known as a "Car Art Reserve" and includes artwork made from auto parts.

NEVADA POTATOES AND BEEF BAKE

1 pound lean ground beef, browned, drained

1 (10¾ ounce) can mushroom soup

1 tablespoon Worcestershire sauce

1 (16 ounce) package frozen vegetables

3 cups hot mash potatoes

Preheat oven to 400 degrees. In 2 quart baking dish mix beef, ½ can soup, Worcestershire sauce, and vegetables. Stir remaining soup into potatoes. Spoon potato mixture over beef mixture. Bake 25 minutes or until hot. ◆Makes 4 servings.

COLORADO BEEF BAKE

1 pound ground beef

1 (1 ounce) package onion soup mix

2 medium tomatoes, chopped

1½ cups uncooked instant rice

1½ cups water

1 cup shredded cheddar cheese

Preheat oven to 400 degrees. In large skillet, brown beef and drain. Stir in soup mix, tomatoes, rice, and water. Mix well. Pour mixture into 2 quart casserole. Cover with aluminum foil. Bake 25 minutes. Uncover, sprinkle cheese over mixture. Bake uncovered 10 minutes. ◆Makes 4 servings.

TEXAS BEEF STEW

▼ *(Crock pot)*

2 pounds beef stew meat

1 (28 ounce) can whole tomatoes, undrained

1 cup small frozen whole onions

1 teaspoon chili powder

1 (1¼ ounce) package taco seasoning mix

1 (15 ounce) can black beans, rinsed, drained

1 (11 ounce) can corn with red and green peppers, drained

In crock pot, combine beef, tomatoes, onions, and chili powder. Cover and cook on low 9 to 10 hours. Stir in taco seasoning, beans, and corn. Cover and cook on high 30 minutes. ◆Makes 6 servings.

SOUTH CAROLINA HEARTY STEW

1 pound ground beef

2 cloves garlic, minced

1 (16 ounce) package frozen vegetables

2 cups southern style hash brown potatoes

1 (14 ounce) jar marinara sauce

1 (10½ ounce) can beef broth

3 tablespoons Worcestershire sauce

In large skillet, brown beef with garlic over medium heat. Drain. Add vegetables, potatoes, sauce, beef broth, and Worcestershire sauce. Simmer on low 15 minutes. ◆Makes 4 to 6 servings.

SKILLET STEW

(Low fat/Low cal)

1 tablespoon vegetable oil

1 teaspoon garlic pepper

1 pound beef sirloin, cut into thin strips

1 (16 ounce) package frozen potatoes, carrots, celery, and onions

1 (12 ounce) jar beef gravy

In medium skillet, heat oil with pepper and beef. Cook over medium heat until brown. Stir in vegetables and gravy. Cover and simmer 10 minutes, stirring often. ◆Makes 4 servings.

Per serving: *Calories–240; Protein–27 gm; Fat–9 gm; Carbohydrates–16 gm; Cholesterol–60 mg; Sodium–670 mg*

SCALLOPED POTATOES AND HAM

▼*(Crock pot)*

1 (28 ounce) bag frozen diced potatoes

1 cup shredded cheddar cheese

1 cup cubed American cheese

1 (10¾ ounce) can celery soup

2 (8 ounce) cartons sour cream

1½ cups cubed uncooked ham

In crock pot, coat with cooking spray. Combine all ingredients in crock pot. Cook on low 5 hours. Stir before serving. Makes 8 servings.

SWEET POTATOES AND HAM

▼ *(Crock pot)*

4 sweet potatoes, sliced in half
   lengthwise
2 pounds boneless ham, cubed
1 cup maple syrup

In crock pot, place potatoes, top with ham. Pour syrup over ham and potatoes. Cover and cook on low 6 to 8 hours. ◆Makes 6 servings.

NOW THAT'S A BAKED POTATO

▼ *(Crock pot)*

8 to 10 medium unpeeled potatoes
2 tablespoons vegetable oil

Pierce potatoes with fork. Place potatoes and oil in large plastic food storage bag. Toss to coat with oil. Wrap potatoes individually in aluminum foil. Place in crock pot. Cover and cook on low heat 8 to 9 hours or until potatoes are tender. ◆Makes 8 servings.

Frey Juan de Padillo, a priest with the Coronado expedition in 1541 is believed to be the first Christian martyr in what is now the U.S. He stayed behind to preach the Catholic faith to the Indians when Coronado returned to Mexico. He was killed near **Lyons, Kansas,** where there is a huge concrete cross honoring him and a museum on the Coronado trail.

Nothing caused more conflict, even resulting in killings, than the Devil's Rope, barbed wire. Cattlemen wanted free range, farmers wanted secure crops. The Barbed Wire Museum in **LaCrosse, Kansas,** displays over 300 kinds of wire, from the first barbed wire in 1867, and includes wire from World War I, the Berlin Wall and the Gulf War.

POTLUCK TATER CASSEROLE
▼ *(Crock pot)*

1 (32 ounce) bag frozen tater tots

1 pound ground beef, browned, drained

½ teaspoon salt

2 (14.5 ounce) cans green beans, drained

1 (10¾ ounce) can cream of mushroom soup

¼ cup milk

In crock pot, line bottom with tater tots. In medium bowl, combine beef, salt, green beans, mushroom soup, and milk. Mix well. Pour over tater tots. Cover and cook on high 3 hours. ◆Makes 6 to 8 servings.

TWO STEP FRIES

1 (32 ounce) package frozen French fry potatoes

1 (10¾ ounce) can cheddar cheese soup

Preheat oven to 400 degrees. On baking sheet, push potatoes into a pile in center. Stir soup in can, spoon over potatoes. Bake 7 minutes or unto hot. Can cook on grill. ◆Makes 6 servings.

GRILLED POUCH POTATOES

1 (10¾ ounce) can cheddar cheese soup
¼ cup milk
½ teaspoon garlic powder
¼ teaspoon onion powder
4 cups frozen steak fries

In large bowl, combine all ingredients. Mix well. Cut 14 inch squares of heavy aluminum foil. Spoon 1 cup mixture onto each square. Bring up sides of foil and double fold. Double fold ends to make a packet. Place packets on grill rack over hot coals. Grill 25 minutes. ◆Makes 4 servings.

DELICIOUS CREAMY POTATOES

▼ *(Crock pot-Low fat/Low cal)*

2½ pounds small red potatoes, quartered
1 (8 ounce) carton sour cream
1 (0.4 ounce) package buttermilk ranch dressing mix
1 (10 ¾ ounce) can cream of mushroom soup

In crock pot, combine all ingredients. Mix well. Cover and cook on high 3½ hours, low 7 hours. ◆Makes 6 servings.

Per servings: *Calories–245; Protein–5 gm; Fat–12 gm; Carbohydrates–30 gm; Sodium–517 mg*

ON THE GRILL POTATOES

2 pounds small red potatoes, cut into 1 inch cubes
1 (1 ounce) package onion soup mix
⅓ cup olive oil
2 tablespoons red wine vinegar
1 garlic clove, diced

In large bowl, combine all ingredients. Mix well. Grease 30x18 inch sheet of heavy aluminum foil. Top with potato mixture. Wrap foil loosely around mixture, sealing edges. Place on another sheet of foil. Seal edges airtight. Grill over medium heat shaking occasionally. Grill 40 to 50 minutes. ◆Makes 4 to 6 servings.

JUICY SWEET POTATOES

(Diabetic)

1 pound sweet potatoes, peeled, cut into ½ inch slices
1 tablespoon cornstarch
1 tablespoon granulate brown sugar substitute
¼ cup unsweetened orange juice
2 tablespoons lemon juice

Preheat oven to 425 degrees. In 1 quart baking dish, coat with cooking spray. Place sweet potatoes. In small bowl, combine cornstarch, brown sugar, orange juice, and lemon juice. Pour over potatoes. Cover and bake for 45 to 50 minutes or until potatoes are tender. ◆Makes 5-½ cup servings.

Per serving: *Exchanges–1 starch, ½ fruit; Calories–105; Carbohydrates–24.4 gm*

MAINE CLASSIC POTATOES

1 (10¾ ounce) can cheddar cheese soup

½ cup milk

¼ teaspoon pepper

½ cup grated Parmesan cheese

4 medium potatoes, cut in 1 inch pieces

1 (2.8 ounce) can French fried onions

Preheat oven to 400 degrees. In greased 2 quart baking dish, combine soup, milk, pepper, and cheese. Stir in potatoes and ½ can onions. Bake 40 minutes or until potatoes are tender. Sprinkle remaining onions over potatoes. Bake 5 minutes more. ◆Makes 4 servings.

TASTY MASHED POTATO BAKE

1 (10¾ ounce) can cheddar cheese soup

⅓ cup sour cream

1 green onion, chopped

3 cups cooked mashed potatoes

Preheat oven to 350 degrees. In 1½ quart casserole, combine all ingredients. Mix well. Bake 30 minutes. ◆Makes 6 to 8 servings.

Greensburg, Kansas, is home of the world's largest hand dug well. It was dug in 1887 and is 32 feet across and 109 feet deep. About a dozen men dug it to furnish water for the city and railroad. It provided water until 1932. If you think you can make it back up again you can go down the 105 steps to the bottom.

Sedan, Kansas is the hometown of one of the world's most famous clowns, the sad faced "Weary Willie", Emmit Kelly. One of his famous routines was sweeping the circle of a spotlight until it narrowed down and out. Your can put your name on an 8" by 10" brick on the Yellow Brick Road, a Main Street sidewalk downtown. Over 10,000 bricks contain names from every state in the Union and 28 foreign countries.

ON THE RUN TUNA BAKE

1 (10¾ ounce) can cream of mushroom soup
½ cup milk
2 (6 ounce) cans tuna, drained
2 cups hot cooked medium noodles
1½ tablespoons butter

Preheat oven to 400 degrees. In 1½ quart casserole, combine all ingredients. Mix well. Bake 25 minutes. ◆Makes 4 servings.

MICROWAVE TUNA MELTS
■*(Microwave)*

1 (6 ounce) can tuna in water, drained
½ cup Miracle Whip®
4 slices American cheese, chopped
½ cup diced celery
¼ cup diced onion
4 rolls

In medium bowl, combine all ingredients, except rolls. Mix well. Fill each roll with ⅓ cup tuna mixture. Place 2 sandwiches on paper towel. Microwave on high 1 minutes or until thoroughly heated. Repeat with remaining sandwiches. ◆Makes 4 servings.

INDIANA TUNA NOODLE BAKE

1 (10¾ ounce) can cream of mushroom soup
½ cup milk
¼ cup shredded cheddar cheese
1 cup cooked peas
2 cups hot cooked egg noodles
2 (6 ounce) cans tuna, drained
2 tablespoons dry breadcrumbs
1 tablespoon margarine or butter, melted

Preheat oven to 375 degrees. In 1½ quart casserole, combine soup, milk, cheese, peas, noodles, and tuna. Bake 25 minutes. In a small bowl, combine breadcrumbs and butter. Mix well. Sprinkle over noodle mixture. Bake 5 minutes more. ◆Makes 4 servings.

FAST WAY MAC AND CHEESE

■*(Microwave)*

1(10¾ ounce) can cheddar cheese soup
1 cup milk
4 cups cooked medium shell macaroni
1 cup shredded cheddar cheese
1 tablespoon butter

In 2 quart microwave safe casserole, combine all ingredients. Cover and cook on high 10 minutes. Uncover and stir. Cook 3 minutes. ◆Makes 6 servings.

No fig leaves in Kansas. In the Garden of Eden in **Lucas, Kansas,** concrete statues of Adam and Eve and the devil are watched over by a giant eye. The sculpture bowed to pressure from modest towns-people and cov-ered Adam's genitalia with a Masonic Lodge apron.

QUICK TRICK BAKE BEANS
▼ *(Crock pot)*

2 (15 ounce) cans pork n beans
¼ cup ketchup
¼ cup maple syrup
½ cup sliced onion
2 tablespoons brown sugar

In crock pot, combine all ingredients. Cover and cook on low 3 to 4 hours. ◆Makes 6 to 8 servings.

DON'T PASS CHILI

½ pound ground beef, browned, drained
2 (14.5 ounce) cans stewed tomatoes, chopped, undrained
1 (15 ounce) can spicy chili beans, undrained
2 teaspoons chili powder

In large saucepan, combine all ingre-dients. Over medium heat, bring to a boil. Reduce heat to low, simmer 5 minutes, stirring occasionally. ◆Makes 6 servings.

TURNPIKE CHILI

1 pound ground beef
½ cup chopped onions
2 (15 ounce) cans chili with beans
1 (10 ounce) can diced tomatoes and green chilies

In medium skillet, brown beef and onion over medium heat. Drain. In large saucepan, combine beef mixture, chili with beans, and tomatoes. Reduce heat and cook 10 minutes. ◆Makes 4 to 6 servings.

SOUTHWEST TACO PIE

1 pound ground beef, browned, drained
1 (10¾ ounce) can tomato soup
1 cup salsa
½ cup milk
8 corn tortillas, cut into 1 inch pieces
1½ cups shredded cheddar cheese

Preheat oven to 350 degrees. In large bowl, combine all ingredients. Pour mixture into 2 quart baking dish. Bake 30 minutes. ◆Makes 4 servings.

Want to try for a world's record? Locals insist that to get good throws you must lick your fingers between throws. That is at the World Championship Cow Chip Throwing Contest in **Beaver, Oklahoma,** each April. The event has drawn international media coverage. What's a cow chip? A dried clump of cow manure–sort of an organic Frisbee.

QUICK CHICKEN ENCHILADAS

1 (24 ounce) carton cottage cheese

2 (12.5 ounce) cans chunk chicken breast, drained

1 (10 ounce) can tomatoes with green chilies

1 (10 ounce) can mild enchilada sauce

10 corn tortillas

2 (1 ounce) package nacho cheese tortilla chips, crushed

3 cups shredded cheddar cheese

Preheat oven to 400 degrees. In large bowl, whip cottage cheese with electric mixer. Add chicken, tomatoes, and enchilada sauce. Mix well. Layer in 2 quart casserole (alternating chicken mixture with corn tortillas). Top with nacho cheese tortilla chips and cheese. Bake 30 minutes. ◆Makes 6 to 8 servings.

OVER THE BOARDER BURRITO WRAPS

■ *(Microwave)*

1 (11¼ ounce) can Fiesta chili beef soup

6 (8 inch) flour tortillas

1 cup shredded cheddar cheese

Spoon 2 tablespoons soup down center of each tortilla. Top with cheese. Fold tortilla around filling. Place seam side down on microwave safe plate. Microwave on high 2 minutes. ◆Makes 6 servings.

NOT JUST BEANS 'N WIENERS

▼ *(Crock pot)*

1 pound wieners, cut into fourths

3 (15 ounce) cans pork n beans in tomato sauce

½ cup ketchup

½ cup diced onion

¼ cup molasses

1 teaspoon mustard

In crock pot, combine all ingredients. Cover and cook on low 5 to 6 hours. ◆Makes 8 serving.

OUTDOOR CHILI DOGS

2 (15 ounce) cans chili without beans

1 (16 ounce) package small hot dogs

1 (8 ounce) package American cheese, cubed

½ cup thick and chunky salsa

In medium heatproof saucepan, combine all ingredients. Mix well. Place on a hot grill or campfire. Cook until hot, stirring frequently. ◆Makes 6 to 8 servings.

One of the largest gun collections in the world is at the J.M. Davis Arms and Historical Museum in **Claremore, Oklahoma.** They display about 15,000 of their over 20,000 firearms. The collection was originally in a hotel run by Mr. Davis, where guns were stacked in rooms. The museum also has other great collections, such as campaign buttons, parlor statuary and animal horns.

Heavener Runestone State Park in **Heavener, Oklahoma,** has a huge sandstone inscribed with what scholars believe is a date–November 11, 1012. This may prove that Norsemen were in Oklahoma 500 years before Coronado.

CAJUN BEANS AND SAUSAGE OVER RICE

2 (15 ounce) cans kidney or pinto beans

1 pound smoked sausage, cut into 2 inch pieces

2 teaspoons Cajun seasoning

In large saucepan, combine all ingredients. Heat over medium heat 20 to 30 minutes. Serve over white rice. ◆Makes 4 to 6 servings.

SCRAMBLED EGGS IN A STYROFOAM CUP

■*(Microwave)*

1 (8 to 10 ounce) Styrofoam cup

1 to 2 eggs

1 tablespoon water or milk

Break eggs into cup. Add salt and pepper to taste. Add water or milk. Whip with a fork. Microwave 1 egg for 25 seconds at high. Stir; microwave 15 to 20 seconds at high. Let stand 1 minute to firm. For 2 eggs, microwave for 30 seconds. Stir; microwave 15 to 25 seconds at high. ◆Makes 1 to 2 servings.

Campfire Blaze

What a bargain—only 15 million dollars! That's what the U.S. paid France for the Louisiana Territory in 1803. It doubled the size of the United States. Thirteen states were carved out of the territory: Arkansas, Colorado, Iowa, Kansas, Louisiana, Minnesota, Missouri, Montana, Nebraska, North Dakota, Oklahoma, South Dakota and Wyoming.

An on-line poll of half a million people rank cities this way. Cleanest—Portland. Dirtiest—New Orleans. Prettiest—San Francisco. Least attractive—Los Angeles. Friendliest—Nashville. Least friendly—Los Angeles. Best nightlife—New Orleans. Worst nightlife—Washington, DC. Best cultural attractions—New York. Worst cultural attractions—Phoenix-Scottsdale.

Seven states have the cardinal as their state bird, six the meadow lark, and five states the mockingbird. Eight states have some kind of pine as their state tree and six a type of oak.

A WINNER CHERRY COFFEECAKE

1 egg
milk
½ cup margarine, softened
1 cup sugar
2 cups flour
2 teaspoons flour
2 teaspoons baking powder
2 (21 ounce) cans cherry pie filling

Preheat oven to 350 degrees. Place egg in measuring cup. Add milk to make one cup. In medium bowl, combine margarine, sugar, flour, and baking powder. Mix well. Pour egg mixture in dry ingredients. Mix well. Pour into 9x14 inch baking pan. Pour cherry pie filling on top of batter. Top with crumb topping (recipe below). Bake for 40 minutes or until lightly brown.

Crumb Topping

1 cup flour
1 cup sugar
½ cup margarine or butter, softened

In medium bowl, combine all ingredients. Mix well. Spread mixture over cherries.

The "Old Round Barn" was built over 100 years ago near **Arcadia, Oklahoma,** by a German farmer who believed its design would make it more resistant to tornadoes. It is refurbished and open to the public traveling Route 66.

SPECIAL BLUEBERRY COFFEE CAKE

1 egg
2¼ cup Bisquick ®
⅓ cup sugar
⅔ cup milk
grated peel of 1 medium lemon
1 cup frozen blueberries

Preheat oven to 400 degrees. In medium bowl, combine Bisquick®, sugar, milk, and lemon peel. Mix well. Add blueberries. Coat round 9 inch baking pan with cooking spray. Pour mixture in pan. Bake 20 to 25 minutes. Drizzle lemon glaze on top (recipe below).

Lemon Glaze

⅔ cup confectioner sugar
3 to 4 teaspoons lemon juice

In small bowl, combine all ingredients. Mix well. Drizzle mixture over coffeecake.

NUTS AND BOLTS STICKY BUNS

2 (7.5 ounce) cans refrigerated biscuits
⅓ cup margarine or butter
½ cup packed brown sugar
½ cup chopped pecans
1 teaspoon cinnamon

Preheat oven to 350 degrees. Melt margarine in 9 inch round baking pan. In small bowl, combine brown sugar, pecans, and cinnamon. Mix well. Sprinkle mixture over melted butter. Arrange biscuits in pan. Biscuits will fit tightly in pan. Bake for 25 to 30 minutes or until golden brown. ◆Makes 8 servings.

BUMPER TO BUMPER CINNAMON ROLLS

¼ cup sugar

½ teaspoon cinnamon

1 (11 ounce) can refrigerated French bread dough

1½ tablespoon margarine or butter

Preheat oven to 350 degrees. In small bowl, combine sugar and cinnamon. Mix well. Grease 9 inch tube pan, set aside. Cut dough into 16 slices, roll into balls. Arrange 12 balls against outer wall of pan. Arrange remaining balls against tube of pan. Brush with margarine. Sprinkle sugar and cinnamon evenly over balls. Bake 20 to 25 minutes or until golden brown. ◆Makes 6 servings.

QUICK FIX DOUGHNUTS

1 (7.5 ounce) can refrigerated biscuits

oil

3 tablespoons sugar

1½ teaspoon cinnamon

Preheat oven to 350 degrees. Make doughnuts by cutting out centers of each biscuit. In deep fat fryer or skillet, drop doughnut in hot oil. Cook until lightly brown. Turn and brown second side. Remove doughnuts, drain on paper towel. Roll in cinnamon and sugar mixture. ◆Makes 4 servings.

Will Rogers, one of America's most beloved humorists, was born in 1879 on a ranch at Oologah, Indian Territory (now **Oklahoma**). He said he was from Claremore, because only an Indian could pronounce Oologah. Open to the public is the house in which he was born on the Dog Iron Ranch at Oolagah, and the Will Rogers Memorial Museum in Claremore has his tomb and a great nine gallery museum depicting his life and achievements.

FRUIT MUFFINS
(Diabetic)

2 cups biscuit mix
¼ cup granulated sugar substitute
¾ cup skim milk
2 tablespoons margarine, melted
12 medium fresh strawberries, chopped

Preheat oven to 400 degrees. In large bowl, combine all ingredients and mix well. Pour mixture into 12 large muffin cups. Bake 20 to 25 minutes. Makes 12 servings.

Per serving: *Exchange–2 bread; Calories–163; Carbohydrates–28 gm*

FROM HOME LEMON MUFFINS

2 cups flour
1 tablespoon baking powder
¼ teaspoon salt
½ cup sugar
2 eggs, beaten
¾ cup milk
2 teaspoons lemon juice
1 teaspoon grated lemon peel
¼ cup butter, melted

Preheat oven to 375 degrees. In large bowl, combine flour, baking powder, salt, and sugar. In medium bowl, combine eggs, milk, lemon juice, lemon peel, and butter. Add to dry mixture. Mix until moistened. Spoon into greased muffin cups. Bake for 15 to 20 minutes.

BLUEBERRY NUT MUFFINS
(Diabetic)

2 cups biscuit mix
¼ cup granulated sugar substitute
¾ cup skim milk
2 tablespoons margarine, melted
1 cup fresh or frozen blueberries
⅓ cup walnuts, chopped

Preheat oven to 400 degrees. In large bowl, combine biscuit mix, sugar, milk, and margarine, mix. Fold in blueberries and walnuts. Pour mixture into 12 large muffin cups. Bake 20 to 25 minutes. ◆Makes 12 servings.

Per serving: *Exchange–1⅓ bread; Calories–112; Carbohydrates–20 gm*

CHOCOLATE CHIP BANANA BREAD

1⅓ cups mashed ripe bananas
¾ cup sugar
¼ cup milk
3 tablespoons oil
½ teaspoon vanilla
3 eggs
2⅔ cups Bisquick®
½ cup semisweet chocolate chips

Preheat oven to 350 degrees. Coat 9x5x3 inch loaf pan with cooking spray. In large bowl, combine bananas, sugar, milk, oil, vanilla, and eggs. Stir in Bisquick® and chocolate chips. Pour mixture into loaf pan. Bake 50 to 60 minutes. Cool 10 minutes, remove from pan.

One of the most famous landmarks on Route 66 is the "Blue Whale," a 50 foot wooden structure at **Catoosa, Oklahoma.** It was built in the 1970's as part of a water park and alligator ranch. It closed in the 1980's and fell into disrepair, but has now been restored to its original condition.

BUMPY CHEESE BREAD

2 cups buttermilk baking mix
½ cup shredded cheese
⅔ cup milk

Preheat oven to 450 degrees. Spray 2½ x 1¼ inch muffin cups with cooking spray. In large bowl, combine all ingredients. Mix well. Pour mixture into muffing cups, half full. Bake 10 to 15 minutes or until lightly brown. ◆Makes 4 servings.

HOT CHEDDAR BREAD SLICES

1 (16 ounce) jar cheddar cheese sauce
1 medium tomato, chopped
5 slices bacon, crisp cooked, crumbled
2 loaves Italian bread, cut into 16 slices

Preheat oven to 350 degrees. In medium bowl, combine cheese sauce, tomatoes, and bacon. Arrange bread slices on baking sheet. Top with mixture evenly on bread slices. Bake 10 minutes. Serve hot. ◆Makes 16 servings.

BUTTER TOPPED BREAD

3 cups self rising flour
2 tablespoons sugar
1 (12 ounce) can beer
¼ cup butter, softened

Preheat oven to 350 degrees. In large bowl, combine flour, sugar, and beer. Mix well. Pour mixture into greased loaf pan. Bake 55 minutes. Remove from oven. Brush top of loaf with soft butter. Return to oven. Bake 5 minutes.

OKLAHOMA INDIAN FRY BREAD

3 cups flour
1¼ teaspoons baking powder
1⅓ cups warm water
¾ cup shortening

In large bowl, combine flour and baking powder. Add warm water. Knead until dough is soft. Pinch off a piece of dough, shape and thin into flat pancake 5 inches in diameter. In medium skillet, heat shortening until hot. Place flat dough in skillet with hot oil. Brown over medium high heat until golden brown on both sides. Drain on paper towels.

One of the top Masonic buildings in the country, the Scottish Rite Masonic Center in Guthrie, was the home of **Oklahoma's** first legislature. The ornate building features rooms designed to reflect different periods of history. Much of the town is on the Historical Register, including a bar where movie actor, Tom Mix, once worked as a bartender.

MASSACHUSETTS BROWN BREAD

1 cup sugar
½ cup canola oil
½ cup molasses
2 eggs, beaten
2 cups all purpose flour
2 teaspoons baking soda
1 teaspoon salt
1 cup boiling water

Preheat oven to 350 degrees. In large mixing bowl, with electric mixer, cream together sugar, oil, molasses, and eggs at medium speed. In small bowl, combine flour, baking soda, and salt. Mix well. Gradually add to mixture, on low speed. Add water and mix. Pour into greased 9x5x2 inch loaf pan. Bake for 45 to 50 minutes. Cool. Makes 1 loaf.

HOT OFF THE FIRE BREAD

⅔ cup wheat flour
⅔ cup flour
⅓ cup powdered milk
1½ teaspoons baking powder
½ teaspoon salt
2½ tablespoons margarine
1½ cups water

In large bowl, combine all ingredients. Mix well. Pour mixture into greased medium iron skillet. Cover and bake over low fire 15 minutes or until done. ◆Makes 4 to 6 servings.

KENTUCKY SPOONBREAD

½ cup margarine, melted

2 eggs

1 cup sour cream

1 (8 ounce) can whole kernel corn

1 (8 ounce) can cream corn

1 (8 ounce) package corn muffin mix

Preheat oven to 350 degrees. In large bowl, beat margarine and eggs. Add sour cream and corn. Add muffin mix. Mix well. Pour into greased 13x9x2 inch pan. Bake for 30 to 40 minutes.

FAST FIX'N ROLLS

4 tablespoons mayonnaise

1 cup milk

¼ teaspoon salt

1 tablespoon melted butter

2 cups self-raising flour

Preheat oven to 350 degrees. In large bowl, combine mayonnaise, milk, salt, and butter. Add flour. Mix well. Pour mixture into greased muffin pan. Bake for 8 to 10 minutes or until golden brown. ◆Makes 8 rolls.

Amarillo, Texas, today produces ninety percent of world's helium. The town sits atop the world's largest known reserves of that gas. A fifty-five foot stainless steel replica of a helium molecule marks that fact.

The mysterious ghost lights of **Marfa, Texas,** have been seen almost nightly since 1883. There is an "official viewing area" about 8 miles west of the small West Texas town on Highway 80. Look southwest toward the mountains, and if you are lucky, you may see a series of shimmering white balls of light in the distance. There has never been an official explanation for them, but theories rang from extraterrestrial to ball lightning to flying bats with radioactive dust on their wings.

BISCUIT ON A STICK

1 (10 count) can biscuits
1 squeeze bottle margarine
1 stick

Roll each biscuit out around a stick. Wrap dough tightly around stick, pinching it as you go to insure that it stays on stick while cooking. Cook over campfire until golden brown. Pull it off stick, pour margarine down hole of biscuit. Keep biscuits in cooler until ready to cook. ◆Makes 5 to 6 servings.

GOOD MORNING BISCUITS

⅔ cup milk
2 cups Bisquick®
1 small egg
⅓ cup crisp cooked diced bacon

Preheat oven to 450 degrees. In large bowl, combine all ingredients. Beat vigorously 20 strokes. Drop dough with spoon onto baking sheet. Bake for 10 to 15 minutes. ◆Makes 12 biscuits.

NEVER FAIL TO PLEASE BISCUITS

4 cups Bisquick®
⅔ cup club soda
1 cup sour cream
1½ stick margarine

Preheat oven to 350 degrees. In large bowl combine, Bisquick, club soda, and sour cream. Mix well. In 2 quart baking pan, melt butter. Roll dough to ½ inch and cut with biscuit cutter. Dip cut dough in butter. Place on baking sheet. Bake 8 to 10 minutes or until golden brown.

DROP BY SPOON BISCUITS

2 cups flour
3 tablespoons baking powder
3½ tablespoons shortening
1 cup milk

Preheat oven to 425 degrees. In large bowl, combine flour and baking powder. Cut in shortening. Add milk. Mix well. Drop by spoonfuls onto baking sheet. Bake 10 to 15 minutes or until golden brown.

Sweetwater, Texas is home of one of the largest rattlesnake roundups in the country each March. If you don't want to join the hunt, you can watch snake handling and venom milking demonstrations, or take part in the rattlesnake meat eating contest.

A life-size statue of Peter Pan is located in **Weatherford, Texas.** It is a tribute to Weatherford native, Mary Martin, who was known for her role of Peter Pan on Broadway and film.

CHEESY TOP BISCUITS

1 (7.5 ounce) can refrigerated biscuits
½ cup melted butter
½ cup cheddar cheese

Preheat oven to 400 degrees. Dip biscuits in butter. Place on baking sheet. Sprinkle cheese on top of biscuits. Bake for 8 to 10 minutes.

YUMMY CINNAMON BISCUIT

1 (7.5 ounce) can refrigerated biscuits
½ cup soft butter
3 tablespoons sugar
½ teaspoon cinnamon

Preheat oven to 400 degrees. On baking sheet, place biscuits spread butter over biscuits. In small bowl, combine sugar and cinnamon. Sprinkle mixture over biscuits. Bake 8 to 10 minutes.

RAISIN TASTING BISCUITS

1 cup raisins
1 cup packed brown sugar
2 (8 count) can refrigerated biscuits
½ cup butter, melted

Preheat oven to 350 degrees. In medium bowl, combine raisins and sugar. Dip each biscuit in butter then dip in raisin mixture. Place on baking sheet. Bake 15 to 20 minutes. ◆Makes 16 biscuits.

SUNNY POPOVERS

(Low fat/Low cal)

2 eggs
1 cup 1% low fat milk
1 tablespoon unsalted butter, melted
1 cup unbleached all purpose white
   flour
½ teaspoon salt

Preheat oven to 400 degrees. Coat 6 muffin cups with butter flavored non-stick spray. In medium bowl, combine all ingredients. Mix do not beat. Pour mixture into cups, fill halfway. Bake 25 minutes. Reduce heat to 350 degrees, bake 10 to 15 minutes or until golden brown. ◆Makes 6 servings.

Per serving: *Calories–125; Protein–6 gm; Fat–4 gm; Carbohydrates–16 gm; Sodium 210 gm*

Everybody is in the movies in **Archer City, Texas.** The movie"Texasville" required 7,000 extras for its crowd scenes, so practically all of the 1,741 residents were in the movie. Larry McMurty, author of "The Last Picture Show" "Texasville", and "Duane's Depressed" used his hometown of Archer City as the basis for his fictional tow of Thalia.

CALIFORNIA CREAM STYLE CORNBREAD

1 cup self rising cornbread
3 eggs
1 cup cream style corn
1 cup sour cream

Preheat oven to 400 degrees. In large bowl, combine all ingredients. Mix well. Pour mixture in greased 2 quart baking pan. Bake 30 to 40 minutes or until golden brown.

COUNTRY FRIED CORNBREAD

2 cups self rising cornbread
2 eggs
½ cup milk
¼ cup shortening, melted

In large bowl, combine all ingredients. Mix well. In medium greased skillet, over medium high heat. Drop mixture by tablespoon in skillet. Cook until golden brown. Turn once. ◆Makes 6 to 8 servings.

OVER THE CAMPFIRE CORNBREAD

1½ cups white cornmeal
½ teaspoon salt
¾ cup boiling water
bacon grease

In medium bowl, combine cornmeal, salt, and boiling water. Mix well. In large skillet with hot bacon grease, drop mixture by tablespoon in skillet. Cook over campfire. Turn once. Cook until golden brown. ◆Makes 4 servings.

A MELLOW CORNBREAD

(Low fat/Low cal)

1 cup cornmeal

1 cup unbleached all purpose white flour

2½ teaspoons baking powder

½ teaspoon baking soda

⅓ cup vegetable oil

¼ cup molasses

1¼ cups buttermilk

2 egg whites

Preheat oven to 400 degrees. Coat 8x8 inch baking pan with cooking spray. In medium bowl, combine cornmeal, flour, baking powder, and soda. Mix well. Add oil, molasses, buttermilk, and egg whites. Mix well. Pour mixture into baking pan. Bake for 20 minutes. ◆Makes 12 servings.

Per serving: *Calories–160; Protein–3 gm; Fat–7 gm; Carbohydrates– 22 gm; Sodium–193 mg*

Want a free steak? You can get it at the Big Texan Steakhouse in **Amarillo, Texas.** The only catch is that you must eat the 72 ounce steak, potato, salad, shrimp cocktail, and roll in one hour. You will be seated on a special stage with a large timer so everyone can monitor your progress. If you fail you pay.

ARIZONA JALAPENO SQUARES

2 eggs
1 cup evaporated milk
½ cup chopped jalapeno
1 cup flour
1 (16 ounce) package cheddar cheese, grated
1 (10 ounce) package Monterey jack cheese, grated

Preheat oven to 350 degrees. In large bowl, combine eggs, milk, and jalapenos. Set aside. In medium bowl, combine flour and cheese. Combine with first mixture. Mix well. Pour into a 13x9 inch baking dish. Bake for 30 minutes. Let cool slightly before cutting into squares. Serve warm. Makes 25 squares.

OLD TIMERS HARDTACK

3 cups flour
1½ teaspoons salt
1½ teaspoons baking powder
1 tablespoon oil
enough water to form stiff dough

Preheat oven to 350 degrees. In large bowl, combine flour, salt, baking powder, and oil. Add water a little at a time, until dough is stiff. Roll out to a ⅜ inch thickness. Cut into 3 inch squares. Make 16 holes in each square on baking sheet. Bake on the middle rack for 40 to 60 minutes. Crackers should not be brown. ◆Makes 10 crackers.

FISH FRY HUSH PUPPIES

1 cup yellow cornmeal
¾ teaspoon baking powder
¼ cup milk
1 egg
¼ cup minced onion
oil

In medium bowl, combine cornmeal and baking powder. Add milk, egg, and onion. Mix well. In medium skillet with hot oil, drop mixture by teaspoon into hot oil for 3 to 5 minutes or until golden brown. Drain on paper towel.

ALABAMA HUSH YOUR MOUTH PUPPIES

2½ cups self rising cornmeal
3 tablespoons self rising flour
1 tablespoon diced onion
1 egg
1 cup milk or water
½ cup oil

In large bowl, combine cornmeal, flour, onion, and egg. Gradually beat in milk. In large skillet heat oil over medium heat until hot. Drop by tablespoon in hot oil. Fry until golden brown and drain on paper towels. ◆Makes16 servings.

"Forbidden Gardens" in **Katy, Texas,** is a replica of the tomb of 3rd century Chinese Emperor Qin Shi Huang, who is credited with creating the nation of China. On its 40 acres are displayed 1/3 scale plexiglass models of the 6,000 terra-cotta soldiers found in Qin's tomb, and a scale replica of the Forbidden City-the palaces where Chinese royalty lived for hundreds of years.

Liberty, Texas, has a bell that was cast by the same English foundry that cast the Liberty Bell in Independence Hall. The original was used as a pattern, but theirs works, unlike the cracked one in Philadelphia. It is rung on special occasions.

WAKE UP TO BREAKFAST

▼ *(Crock pot)*

1½ cups oatmeal

3 cups water

2 cups sliced apples

½ teaspoon cinnamon

In crock pot, coat with cooking spray. Combine all ingredients in cock pot. Cover and cook on low 8 to 9 hours. Can use ½ cup raisins. ◆Makes 4 to 6 servings.

FREEDOM TOAST

3 eggs

2 tablespoons milk

¼ teaspoon cinnamon

2 tablespoon oil

6 slices bread

In medium bowl, combine eggs, milk, and cinnamon. Mix well. in large skillet with oil, heat over medium high until hot. Dip bread slices in egg mixture, coat well. Place in skillet, brown on both sides. ◆Makes 3 to 6 servings.

BEE SWEET PANCAKES

2 cups Bisquick®
1 cup milk
2 tablespoons honey
1 egg

In large bowl, combine all ingredients. Mix well. Coat large skillet with cooking spray. Heat over medium high heat. Pour ¼ cup mixture at a time in hot skillet. Cook until edges are dry. Turn and cook until golden brown. Serve with butter and syrup.

HOBO PANCAKE SYRUP

2 cups packed brown sugar
1 cup water
1 tablespoon butter
½ teaspoon maple flavoring

In medium saucepan, combine all ingredients. Over medium heat, bring to a boil. Boil for 2 to 3 minutes.

UTAH HOMEMADE PANCAKE SYRUP

¾ cup honey
½ cup butter or margarine
½ teaspoon cinnamon

In 1 quart saucepan, combine all ingredients. Heat over low heat until hot.

The tallest stone monument in the world is the San Jacinto Monument near **Houston, Texas**. At 570 feet it is fifteen feet taller than the Washington Monument. It marks the spot of the final battle for Texas' independence from Mexico.

One of the most famous signatures of the American West is not in a museum. It is in a glass case near the top of a 150 foot sandstone outcrop called Pompys Pillar overlooking the Yellowstone River in Southwest **Montana.** William Clark of the famous Lewis and Clark expedition carved his name in July 25, 1806 as he was homeward bound. It is the only written evidence the group left of their 2 year, 4 month, 10 day journey.

SELF RISING FLOUR

1 cup flour
1½ teaspoons baking powder
½ teaspoon salt

In small bowl, combine all ingredients. Mix well. ◆Makes 1 cup.

SELF RISING CORNMEAL

1 cup cornmeal
1½ teaspoons baking powder
½ teaspoon salt

In small bowl, combine all ingredients. Mix well. ◆Makes 1 cup.

Hitting the High-lights

Cakes

Pies

Cookies

Desserts

Candy

TRIVA

The Underground Railroad was a series of secret hiding places for slaves fleeing their owners in the South heading for freedom in the North, usually Canada, between 1790 and the Civil War. Some restored stops include: Paxton Inn—Washington, Kentucky; old Eleutherian College building—Lancaster, Indiana; Pearl Sheton's house—Hopedale, Ohio; Owen Lovejoy Homestead—Princeton, Illinois; Gerrit Smith Estate—Petersboro, New York; Milton House Museum—Milton, Wisconsin.

Thirsty? To order a carbonated beverage in the Midwest, in the Pacific Northwest and around the Great Lakes make like a local and ask for "pop". On the East Coast, West Coast and in the South order a "soda". Some people refer to any carbonated drink as a "cola" regardless of the flavor.

Spanish Moss is not Spanish and is not a moss, but it grows almost anywhere in the South where there is warm air and high humidity. Legend has it that, as was traditional, an Indian princess cut her hair on her wedding day and hung it on an oak tree. Unfortunately the couple were killed in an enemy raid on the day they were married and buried under the oak tree. Her hair turned gray, started to grow and has been spreading among the trees ever since.

When you think of gold discoveries you think of California or the Rocky Mountains. The first gold found in America was in Cabarrus County, North Carolina, in 1799. A 12 year old found a 17 pound chunk he sold for $3.50. Gold was also discovered in Sahlonega, Georgia. This gold strike helped push the Cherokee Indians off their native lands.

STRAWBERRY PATCH CREAM PIE

(Low Fat/Low cal)

1 cup sliced strawberries

1½ packets sweetener

1 (8 ounce) pie crust, baked

1 (8 ounce) package reduced fat cream cheese, softened

⅓ cup vanilla flavored light nonfat yogurt

6 packets sweetener

1 tablespoon lemon juice

6 strawberries

In small bowl, combine strawberries and 1½ packets sweetener. Mix well. Let set 5 minutes. Pour mixture into pie crust. In medium bowl, combine cream cheese, yogurt, 6 packets sweetener, and lemon juice. Beat until smooth and fluffy. Spread over sliced strawberries. Cut 6 strawberries in half. Arrange berries around outer edge of pie crust. ◆Makes 8 servings.

Per serving: *Calories–185; Protein–4 gm; Fat–9 gm; Carbohydrates–13 gm; Cholesterol–20 mg; Sodium–144 mg*

JUST TOO COOL BERRY PIE

1 (14 ounce) can sweetened condensed milk

½ cup lemon juice

2 cups raspberries or blackberries

1 (8 ounce) tub frozen whipped topping

1 (9 inch) graham cracker pie crust

In large bowl, combine milk and lemon juice. Add berries. Fold in whipped topping. Spoon mixture into crust. Chill until set. ◆Makes 8 servings.

DISTRICT OF COLUMBIA APPLE PIE

½ cup margarine, melted

1¼ cups sugar

1 teaspoon cinnamon

1 egg, beaten

3 cups chopped apples

1 (9 inch) unbaked pie crust

Preheat oven to 400 degrees. In large bowl, combine margarine, sugar, cinnamon, and egg. Mix well. Add apples. Mix well. Pour mixture in pie crust. Bake 10 minutes. Reduce heat to 350 degrees. Bake 40 minutes. ◆Makes 8 servings.

CRUISE AMERICA PUMPKIN PIE

2 eggs

½ cup sugar

1 teaspoon cinnamon

½ teaspoon salt

½ teaspoon ginger

⅛ teaspoon cloves

1 (15 ounce) can pumpkin

1 (12 ounce) can evaporated milk

1 (9 inch) unbaked pie crust

Preheat oven to 425 degrees. In medium bowl, combine all ingredients. Mix well. Pour mixture into pie crust. Bake 15 minutes. Reduce heat to 350 degrees. Bake 45 minutes. Cool. ◆Makes 8 servings.

WITHOUT THE CRUST COCONUT PIE

¼ cup margarine

¾ cup sugar

2 eggs

1 cup milk

¼ cup self rising flour

1 (3½ ounce) can flaked coconut

Preheat oven to 350 degrees. In large bowl, combine margarine and sugar. Mix well. Add eggs, one at a time, mixing after each addition. Add milk and flour. Mix well. Add coconut. Pour into lightly greased 9 inch pie pan. Bake 40 minutes. ◆Makes 8 servings.

FLUFFY LEMONADE PIE

1 (6 ounce) can frozen lemonade

1 pint vanilla ice cream

1½ cup frozen whipped topping

1 (9 inch) graham cracker crust

In large bowl, combine all ingredients. Mix well. Pour mixture into graham cracker crust and chill. ◆Makes 8 servings.

In 1886 in **Montana** a buffalo was shot, stuffed and displayed at the Smithsonian Museum in Washington, DC. It was used as the model for the buffalo nickel and for postage stamps. In 1970 it was returned home and is on display at the Museum of the Upper Missouri in Ft. Benton, Montana.

NORTH CAROLINA PECAN PIE

¾ cup dark corn syrup

½ cup packed brown sugar

4 tablespoons butter or margarine, melted

1 teaspoon vanilla

3 large eggs

¾ cup pecan halves

1 cup chopped pecans

1 (9 inch) unbaked pie crust

Preheat oven to 425 degrees. In large bowl, combine syrup, brown sugar, butter, vanilla, and eggs. Mix well. Add pecans, mix. Pour mixture into pie shell. Bake 45 to 50 minutes. ◆Makes 8 servings.

PEANUT BUTTER CHOCOLATE PIE

2 (1 ounce) squares semisweet baking chocolate

1 (14 ounce) can sweetened condensed milk

¼ cup creamy peanut butter

1 (8 ounce) tub frozen whipped topping

1 (9 inch) graham cracker pie crust

In large bowl, place chocolate. Microwave on high 15 to 20 seconds or until chocolate has melted. Add milk and peanut butter. Mix well. Fold in whipped topping. Spoon into crust and freeze. ◆Makes 8 servings.

CHOCOLATE ESCAPE PIE

1 (8 ounce) package cream cheese, softened
1 (14 ounce) can sweetened condensed milk
6 ounces semisweet chocolate, melted
1½ cups whipped topping
1 (9 inch) graham cracker pie crust

In large bowl, beat cream cheese until smooth. Add milk and chocolate. Beat until creamy. Fold in whipped topping. Pour mixture into graham cracker pie crust. Cover and freeze until firm. To serve, place pie in refrigerator for 30 minutes. ◆Makes 8 servings.

MAKE MY DAY PECAN PIE

⅔ cup sugar
⅓ cup butter, melted
1 cup corn syrup
½ teaspoon salt
3 eggs
1 cup broken pecans
1 cup semisweet chocolate chips
1 (9 inch) unbaked pie crust

Preheat oven to 375 degrees. In large bowl, combine sugar, butter, syrup, salt, and eggs. Beat well. Add pecans and chips, mix. Pour mixture into pie crust. Cover edge of crust with tin foil. Bake 35 minutes. Take off tin foil and bake 15 minutes. Tin foil helps keep edges of crust from over browning. ◆Makes 8 servings.

COAST TO COAST PINEAPPLE CAKE

½ cup butter or margarine, melted
1 cup packed brown sugar
1 (20 ounce) can pineapple slices, drained
8 maraschino cherries, cut in half
1 box moist deluxe pineapple supreme cake mix
whipped cream

Preheat oven to 350 degrees. In 13x9 inch baking pan, pour butter. Sprinkle sugar over butter. Arrange pineapple slices and maraschino cherries on sugar mixture. Prepare cake mix as directed on package. Pour over fruit. Bake 50 minutes. Let stand 5 minutes. Invert onto serving plate or cookie sheet. Serve warm with whip cream. ◆Makes 12 to 16 servings.

UPSIDE DOWN CHOCOLATE CAKE

1½ cups flaked coconut
1½ cups chopped pecans
1 box deluxe chocolate cake mix
1 (8 ounce) package cream cheese, softened
½ cup butter or margarine, melted
3¾ cups confectioners sugar

Preheat oven to 350 degrees. In 13x9 inch baking pan, grease and flour. Spread coconut evenly on bottom of pan. Sprinkle with pecans. In large bowl prepare cake as directed on package. Pour over coconut and pecans. In medium bowl combine cream cheese and butter. Beat at low speed with electric mixer. Add sugar. Beat until smooth. Drop by spoonfuls evenly over cake batter. Bake 45 to 50 minutes. Cool to warm. Turn cake upside down onto serving plate. ◆Makes 12 to 15 servings.

SO EASY CHOCOLATE CAKE

½ cup miniature semisweet
  chocolate chips
⅓ cup packed brown sugar
⅓ cup chopped pecans
1 box devil's food cake mix

Preheat oven to 350 degrees. In 13x9x2 inch baking pan, coat with cooking spray. In medium bowl. Combine chocolate chips, brown sugar, and pecans. Mix well, set a side. Prepare cake mix as directed on package. Pour into baking pan. Sprinkle chocolate chip mixture over batter. Bake 30 to 35 minutes. Cool. Frost with your favorite frosting. ◆Makes 15 servings.

MIRACLE WHIP®
CHOCOLATE CAKE

Busy Women's Cookbook

1 cup Miracle Whip®
3 eggs
1 box devil's food cake mix
1⅓ cups water

Preheat oven to 350 degrees. In large bowl, combine all ingredients. Mix well. Pour mixture into greased 9x13 inch cake pan. Bake for 35 to 40 minutes.

Southwest of **Great Falls, Montana,** at Ulm, Ukm Pishkun State Park off I-15 has one of the largest buffalo jumps in the world. Over these cliffs, which stretch over one mile and are over 30 feet high, prehistoric people between 900 and 1500 A.D. stampeded herds of bison. Below the cliffs compacted bones have been uncovered 13 feet deep.

John Quigley single-handedly built buildings for thirty-three years to create a full size replica of an Old West town, Frontier Town near **Helena, Montana.** It includes a general store, brewery, church and restaurant.

ANGEL IN MY KITCHEN CAKE

1 box Angel food cake mix
1¾ teaspoons cinnamon, divided
1½ cups frozen whipped topping

Preheat oven to 350 degrees. Prepare cake as directed on package. In 10 inch tube pan, spoon one third of batter. Sprinkle 1½ teaspoons cinnamon over batter. Top with remaining cake batter. Bake and cool following package directions. In medium bowl, combine whipped topping and ¼ teaspoon cinnamon, mix. Serve with cake. ◆Makes 12 servings.

PENNSYLVANIA CHEESE CAKE

■*(Microwave)*

1 (8 ounce) package cream cheese
½ cup sugar
1 egg
1 teaspoon vanilla
1 (9 inch) graham cracker crust
1 (20 ounce) can cherry pie filling

In medium microwave safe bowl, place cream cheese. Microwave at medium high 1 minute. Combine with sugar, egg, and vanilla. Beat until well blended. Pour into graham cracker crust in glass pie plate. Microwave at medium high for 5 minutes. Cool and spread with cherry pie filling. ◆Makes 6 to 8 servings.

ICE CREAM SANDWICH CAKE

16 ice cream sandwich bars
1 (8 ounce) tub whipped topping
1½ cups hot fudge sauce, cold

In 9x13 inch cake pan, layer 8 ice cream sandwiches. Spread one half of fudge sauce over ice cream sandwiches. Top with one half of whipped topping. Layer 8 more ice cream sandwiches, fudge sauce, and whipped topping. Freeze. Cut into bars. ◆Makes 8 servings.

NO FLOUR PEANUT BUTTER COOKIES

1 cup creamy peanut butter
1 cup packed light brown sugar
1 large egg
¾ cup milk chocolate chips
¼ cup sugar

Preheat oven to 350 degrees. In medium bowl, combine peanut butter, brown sugar, and egg, mix. Add chips, mix well. Roll heaping tablespoonfuls of dough into 1½ inch balls. Place balls 2 inches apart on ungreased cookie sheets. Dip fork into sugar, press criss cross onto each ball, flatten to ½ inch thickness. Bake 12 minutes or until set. Let set 2 minutes. Remove cookies to wire racks. ◆Makes 2 dozen cookies.

Cut Bank, Montana, often has the lowest temperature in the continental United States. To showcase this fact, the town has the world's largest penguin statue. The concrete sculpture is 27 feet tall and weighs 10,000 pounds.

MOTORHOME BAR COOKIES

2 cups graham cracker crumbs
1 cup semisweet chocolate chips
1 cup flaked coconut
¾ cup chopped walnuts
1 (14 ounce) can sweetened condensed milk

Preheat oven to 350 degrees. Coat 13x9 inch baking pan with cooking spray, set aside. In medium bowl, combine crumbs, chips, coconut, and walnuts, mix. Add milk, mix well. Spread batter evenly into baking pan. Bake 15 to 18 minutes or until edges are golden brown. ◆Makes 20 bars.

EASY FIXED COOKIES

1 box chocolate cake mix
2 eggs
½ cup chopped walnuts
⅓ cup oil

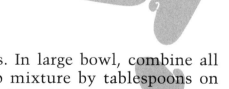

Preheat oven to 350 degrees. In large bowl, combine all ingredients. Mix well. Drop mixture by tablespoons on ungreased cookie sheet. Bake 10 to 12 minutes.

QUICK COOKIES FOR CAMPING

1 cup sugar
1 cup corn syrup
1¾ cups peanut butter
6 cups Post Toasties®

In large pan, combine sugar and syrup, bring to a boil over medium heat. Add peanut butter and Post Toasties. Mix well. Drop by teaspoonful on waxed paper. Cool.

TOO HOT FOR BAKED COOKIES

2 cups sugar
¼ cup butter
½ cup milk
2½ tablespoons cocoa
1 teaspoon vanilla
½ cup peanut butter
3 cups oats

In large saucepan, combine sugar, butter, milk, and cocoa over medium heat, boil 1 minute. Remove from heat. Add vanilla, peanut butter, and oats. Mix well. Drop by tablespoonful on waxed paper. Let cool.

PACK-N-GO COOKIES

⅓ cup cocoa
¼ cup sugar
2 cups miniature marshmallows
1 cup peanut butter chips
½ cup butter
1¼ cups quick cooking oats

In medium saucepan, combine cocoa and sugar. Add marshmallows, peanut butter chips, and butter. Heat over medium heat until mixture is smooth. Remove from heat. Stir in oats. Drop by heaping teaspoons on waxed paper. If mixture is to soft, let stand 2 minutes before you drop mixture. Chill. ◆Makes 24 cookies.

The high-climbing 68 mile Beartooth Scenic Highway begins at **Red Lodge, Montana,** a 1890 coal mining town, and is known for its views and wild-flowers. It leads through Red Rock Canyon to Gardner Lake to Beartooth Pass, one of America's highest roads (10,947 feet). Charles Kuralt once called this "the most beauti-ful drive in America". It ends in Silver Gate, just a few miles from Yellowstone National Park.

The wind blows so regularly at **Medicine Gap, Wyoming,** that residents joke that if it stopped blowing, everyone would fall down because they are so used to leaning into the wind. Electricity is generated by wind generators that provide electricity to several Colorado communities. The world's largest wind turbine-263 feet tall-was built in the 1970's. It is no longer functioning, but nine smaller turbines-131 and 147 feet tall-take advantage of the energy of the wind.

HAVE A CHOCOLATE CHIP COOKIE

(Low fat/Low cal)

⅓ cup margarine, softened

1 egg

1 teaspoon vanilla

8 packets sweetener

⅓ cup packed light brown sugar

¼ cup all purpose flour

½ teaspoon baking soda

¼ teaspoon salt

½ cup semisweet chocolate chips

Preheat oven to 350 degrees. In medium bowl, combine margarine, egg, and vanilla. Beat with electric mixer until fluffy. Add sweetener and brown sugar, beat until blended. In small bowl, combine flour, baking soda, salt. Mix well. Add to mixture. Stir in chocolate chips. Drop mixture by teaspoonfuls onto ungreased baking sheet. Bake 8 to 10 minutes or until light golden brown. ◆Makes 2 dozen.

Per serving (1 cookie): *Calories–67; Protein–1 gm; Fat–4 gm; Carbohydrates–8 gm; Cholestero–16 mg; Sodium–8mg*

DROP AND BAKE SUGAR COOKIES

(Low fat/Low cal)

1⅓ cups all purpose flour
¾ teaspoon baking powder
¼ teaspoon salt
½ cup butter, softened
1 cup sugar
1 large egg
1 teaspoon vanilla

Preheat oven to 350 degrees. In small bowl, combine flour, baking powder, and salt. Mix well. In large bowl, combine butter, sugar, egg, and vanilla. Beat until blended. Add flour mixture. Mix well. On ungreased cookie sheet, drop mixture by heaping teaspoonfuls 2 inches apart. Bake 10 to 12 minutes or until browned around edges. ◆Makes 40 cookies.

Per serving (1 cookie): *Calories–54; Protein–1 gm; Fat–2 gm; Carbohydrates–8 gm; Cholesterol–11 mg; Sodium–46 mg*

Near **Kemmerer, Wyoming,** the Pittsburg and Midway Coal Mine, with a depth of 800 feet, is the largest open pit coal mine in the United States. The mine is capable of producing 4.2 million tons of coal a year, and is located in an area believed to contain up to 500 million tons of coal.

SWEET MACAROONS

(Low fat/Low cal)

3 cups flaked unsweetened coconut

¾ cup sugar

4 large egg whites

¼ teaspoon salt

1 teaspoon vanilla

⅛ teaspoon almond extract

Preheat oven to 325 degrees. In large bowl, combine all ingredients. Mix well. Coat cookie sheet with cooking spray. Drop mixture by rounded teaspoonfuls 1 inch apart. Bake 25 minutes or until lightly golden.

Per serving (1 cookie): *Calories–41; Protein–1 gm; Fat–2 gm; Carbohydrates–6 gm; Cholesterol–0 mg; Sodium–32 mg*

COOK DON'T BAKE BROWNIES

1 (14 ounce) can sweetened condensed milk

2 (1 ounce) squares unsweetened chocolate, cut up

1 teaspoon vanilla

2 cups chocolate cookie crumbs

¼ cup chopped nuts

In medium saucepan, combine milk and chocolate. Cook over medium heat until mixture starts to boil. Mix, reduce heat to low, cook 3 minutes more. Remove from heat. Add vanilla and cookie crumbs. Spread evenly in greased 8 inch square pan. Sprinkle nuts over mixture. Press down gently with a spoon on nuts. Cover and chill. ◆Makes 24 brownies.

MAKE-N-TAKE BROWNIES

¾ cup butter or margarine, melted

1½ cups sugar

1½ teaspoons vanilla

3 eggs

¾ cup flour

½ cup cocoa

½ teaspoon baking powder

½ teaspoon salt

Preheat oven to 350 degrees. In 8 inch square baking pan, coat with cooking spray. In large bowl, combine butter, sugar, and vanilla. Add eggs. Mix well. In medium bowl, combine flour, cocoa, baking powder, and salt. Add to egg mixture. Mix well. Spread batter into baking pan. Bake 40 to 45 minutes. Use frosting of your choice. ◆Makes 16 brownies.

SOUTH DAKOTA CHERRY BROWNIES

1 box chocolate cake mix

1 cup prepared chocolate pudding

4 tablespoons melted butter

1 egg

¼ cup honey

1 teaspoon vanilla

1 cup canned pitted tart red cherries, drained, halved

Preheat oven to 350 degrees. In 10x10 inch baking pan, coat with cooking spray. In large bowl, combine cake mix, pudding, butter, egg, honey, and vanilla. Mix well. Pour mixture in baking pan. Sprinkle cherries over top of batter. Bake 20 to 25 minutes. Cool. Cut into squares. ◆Makes 12 servings.

CRISPY TREATS BARS

(Diabetic)

3 tablespoons margarine

⅓ cup packed granulated brown sugar substitute

2 cups miniature marshmallows

4 cups oven toasted rice cereal

2 cups whole wheat flake cereal

In large saucepan, melt margarine over medium heat. Add brown sugar and marshmallows, cook and stir until marshmallows are melted. Remove from heat. Stir in cereals. Mix well. Coat 13x9x2 inch baking pan. Press mixture evenly into pan. Cool. Cut into 3x2 inch bars. ◆Makes 18 bars.

Per servings (1 bar): *Exchanges–1 starch; Calories–72; Carbohydrates–13 gm*

SPEEDBUMP CHEWY BARS

■*(Microwave)*

½ cup margarine

½ cup packed brown sugar

½ cup honey

2 cups quick oats

1 cup chocolate chips

½ cup peanut butter

In 8 inch microwave dish, combine margarine, sugar and honey. Microwave on high 1 minute. Mix well. Add oats, mix. Spread mixture evenly into pan. Microwave on medium high for 5 minutes or until bubbly. Cool. In small bowl, combine chocolate chips and peanut butter. Microwave for 2 minutes. Mix until smooth. Spread over mixture. Chill. Cut into squares.

YUMMY PEACH DESSERT

(Diabetic)

1½ cups fresh raspberries

2 tablespoons granulated sugar substitute

2 teaspoons lemon juice

1 (16 ounce) can peach halves, drained

1½ cups sugar free vanilla nonfat ice cream

In small bowl, combine raspberries, sugar, and lemon juice. Mix well. Let stand 10 minutes. Spoon mixture into 6 dessert dishes. Place 1 peach half cut side up on raspberries. Spoon ¼ cup ice cream on each peach. ◆Makes 6 servings.

Per serving: *Exchanges–1 starch, ½ fruit; Calories–95; Carbohydrates–21.7 gm*

QUICK TRICK PEACH CRISP

2 (15¼ ounce) cans sliced peaches

2 individual serving packages about (1.6 ounce) each cinnamon and spice instant oatmeal, uncooked

⅓ cup flour

⅓ cup butter, melted

Preheat oven to 425 degrees. In 8 inch square baking dish, pour peaches. In medium bowl, combine oatmeal, flour, and butter. Mix well. Sprinkle mixture over peaches. Bake 15 minutes or until golden brown. Serve warm over ice cream. ◆Makes 6 servings.

HIGHLIGHTS PEACH CRISP
(Diabetic)

1 (16 ounce) can sliced peaches, drained

2 tablespoons granulated sugar substitute

1 teaspoon cornstarch

¼ cup low fat granola, without raisins

In medium bowl, combine peaches, sugar, and cornstarch. Mix well. Pour into 8 inch square baking pan. Sprinkle granola over peach mixture. Bake 15 to 18 minutes. Makes 2 servings

Per serving: *Exchanges–½ starch, 1–fruit; Calories–100; Carbohydrates–22.9 gm*

JUST LIKE PEACH COBBLER
▼ *(Crock pot)*

⅓ cup buttermilk baking mix

⅔ cup quick oats

½ cup packed brown sugar

1 teaspoon cinnamon

4 (canned or fresh) cups peaches

½ cup peach juice or water

In medium bowl, combine buttermilk baking mix, oats, sugar, and cinnamon. Mix well. Coat crock pot with cooking spray. Add mixture. Cover mixture with peaches and juice. Cover and cook on low 5 hours. Take off lid. Cook 20 minutes. ◆Makes 6 servings.

MISSOURI PEACH COBBLER

4 cups peeled, sliced, peaches
1 cup blackberries
¾ cups sugar
1 teaspoon cornstarch
1¼ cups self rising flour
2 tablespoons sugar
1 cup milk
½ cup butter or margarine, melted

Preheat oven to 400 degrees. In large bowl, combine peaches, berries, sugar, and cornstarch. Mix well. Set aside. In medium bowl, combine flour, sugar, milk, and butter. Mix well. Pour mixture over fruit. Bake 45 to 50 minutes. ◆Makes 6 to 8 servings.

GEORGIA FRIED PEACHES

2 tablespoons butter or margarine
6 fresh peaches, peeled, halved, seeded
¼ cup packed brown sugar
1 teaspoon cinnamon
whipped topping

In large skillet melt butter then add peaches, cut side up. Sprinkle brown sugar over peaches. Cover and cook over low heat 10 minutes or until tender. Remove from heat. Sprinkle cinnamon over peaches. Serve with whipped topping. ◆Makes 4 servings.

You may have to take a number, stand in a line that snakes from an early 1900's whitewashed building and rub shoulders with people from all around the world to get a world-famous malt or shake at Yellowstone Drug in **Shoshomi, Wyoming.** Hand mixed shakes from hard ice cream in 59 flavors keep the tourists coming. Their record is 727 shakes (one every 44 seconds) in one day.

Who built the Medicine Wheel near **Lovell, Wyoming?** No one knows for sure, but it is a sacred place to a number of Indian tribes. Built between A.D. 1200 and 1700, it is made of a central pile of rocks with 28 spokes of rocks stretching out about 40 feet to an outer ring of rocks. A gravel road leads up into the Bighorn Mountains to the location.

HAWAII PINEAPPLE DESSERT

■*(Microwave)*

4 cups pineapple chunks

1 (11 ounce) can mandarin oranges,drained

⅓ cup packed brown sugar

¼ cup rum

2 tablespoons margarine or butter

⅓ cup shredded coconut, toasted

In 1½ quart casserole, combine pineapple, oranges, brown sugar, rum, and butter. Mix well. Cover and microwave on high 5 minutes or until bubbly. Mix well. Sprinkle coconut over mixture. Serve warm. ◆Makes 6 servings.

FLORIDA ORANGE DESSERT

3 (11 ounce) cans mandarin oranges, drained

⅓ cup sugar

⅔ cup shredded coconut

In a serving dish, arrange orange sections. Sprinkle sugar then coconut over orange sections. Cover and chill. ◆Makes 4 servings.

DELIGHTFUL FRUIT COCKTAIL

1 (15 ounce) can fruit cocktail, undrained

1 (4 ounce) box instant vanilla pudding mix

½ cup miniature marshmallows

½ cup chopped nuts

In large bowl, combine fruit cocktail and pudding. Chill. Just before serving add marshmallows. Top with nuts. ◆Makes 4 to 6 servings.

HOT CHERRY DELIGHT

▼ *(Crock pot)*

1 (21 ounce) can cherry pie filling

1 bow yellow cake mix

½ cup butter, melted

In crockpot, coat with cooking spray. Pour cherry pie filling in bottom. In medium bowl, combine cake mix and butter. Mix until crumbly. Sprinkle mixture over cherry filling. Cover and cook on low 4 hours on high 2 hours. Cool. Serve with ice cream. ◆Makes 8 servings

Douglas, Wyoming, is the Jackalope Capital of the World. The city actually owns the trademark of the mythical creature and the town is decorated with its image. The town plaza has an eight foot statue of a jackalope–a rabbit with antlers, a cross between the jackrabbit and the antelope. Beware the tall tales of the town residents.

In late October each year 7,500 elk move into the lower elevation of the National Elk Refuge in **Jackson Hole, Wyoming,** and stay until spring, then return to Grand Teton and Yellowstone National Parks. Wolves, trumpeter swans and 500 bison also winter there.

CROCK POT CARAMEL APPLES

▼ *(Crock pot)*

2 (14 ounce) packages caramels
¼ cup water
8 medium apples

In crockpot, combine caramels and water. Cover and cook on high 1 to 1½ hours stirring frequently. Insert stick in stem of each apple. Dip apples in mixture, coat entire surface. Place on greased waxed paper to cool. ◆Makes 8 servings.

HEALTHY ORANGE FRUIT POPS

1½ cups fresh squeezed orange juice
1½ cups apple juice
4 (7 or 8 ounce) paper cups
4 plastic spoons

In medium container, combine orange juice and apple juice. Pour into paper cups. Freeze until almost firm. Insert spoons in cups. Freeze until firm. To serve, allow pops to stand at room temperature for a few minutes. Peel paper from cups. Makes 4 servings.

CARAMEL TASTING CUSTARD

(Diabetic)

1 tablespoon sugar free maple flavored syrup
1 egg
½ cup evaporated milk
⅓ cup water
1 tablespoon granulated sugar replacement
1 teaspoon vanilla

Preheat oven to 350 degrees. In two custard cups divide maple syrup evenly in cups. In medium bowl, combine egg, milk, water, sugar, and vanilla. Beat until well blended. Pour mixture into custard cups. Place cups in shallow pan with 1 inch of water. Bake 50 minutes. ◆Makes 2 servings.

Per serving: *Exchanges–1 skim milk; Calories–85; Carbo-hydrates–7 gm*

QUICK WAY RICE PUDDING

■*(Microwave)*

2 cups milk
½ cup minute rice
1 (4 serving) box vanilla pudding mix, not instant

In 1quart casserole, combine all ingredients. Microwave on high 5 to 6 minutes. Stir twice while cooking. Pour into Styrofoam cups or dishes. Chill. ◆Makes 3 to 4 servings.

The town of **Dillon, Colorado,** (pop. 802) can't make up its mind where it wants to be. It was founded at the site of a trading post on the Snake River in 1883. In order to be closer to the railroad it moved across the river, then moved again to be between the three rivers, the Blue, the Ten Mile and the Snake. In 1961 to avoid being flooded by the Dillon Reservoir, it had to move to its present location on the shore of the reservoir.

RHODE ISLAND BAKED CUSTARD

4 eggs, slightly beaten
3½ cups milk
¾ cup sugar
1 teaspoon vanilla
1 teaspoon nutmeg

Preheat oven to 350 degrees. In large bowl, combine eggs, milk, sugar, and vanilla. Mix well. Pour mixture into 8 custard cups. Sprinkle nutmeg over mixture in custard cups. Place cups in shallow baking pan. Add 1 inch hot water to pan. Bake 40 to 45 minutes. Chill. ◆Makes 8 servings.

HAVING A PARTY ICE CREAM

6 eggs
1 cup sugar
4 tablespoons white corn syrup
1 (15 ounce) can sweetened
   condensed milk
1 teaspoon vanilla
milk

In large bowl, combine eggs and sugar. Mix well with electric mixer. Add syrup, condensed milk, and vanilla. Blend and pour into freezer container. Add milk to within 4 inches from top of container. Freeze according to freezer directions, then let stand 1 hour before serving. ◆Makes 8 servings.

CHOCOLATE CHIP ICE CREAM

2 cups sugar

⅓ cup cocoa

4 cups light cream

6 eggs, beaten

4 cups whipping cream

1 tablespoon vanilla

2 cups milk chocolate chips

In large saucepan, combine sugar and cocoa. Add light cream. Cook over medium heat, stirring constantly, until bubbly. Add eggs. Cook 3 minutes or until mixture is slightly thickened. Remove from heat. Stir in whipping cream and vanilla. Cover and chill. Pour mixture in cylinder of 4 or 5 quart ice cream freezer. Freeze according to manufacturer's directions. Stir in chips. Ripen 4 hours. ◆Makes 3 quarts.

SWEET TREAT FUDGE

3 cups semisweet chocolate chips

1 (14 ounce) can sweetened
  condensed milk

1 cup chopped nuts

1½ teaspoons vanilla

Line 9 inch square pan with waxed paper. In large saucepan, combine chocolate chips and milk over low heat. Cook until chocolate chips have melted. Remove from heat. Add nuts and vanilla. Mix well. Spread mixture evenly into prepared pan. Chill until firm. Cut into squares. Keep fresh in refrigerator. ◆Makes 2 pounds.

GIMME A BRAKE FUDGE

1 (16 ounce) semisweet chocolate, chopped
1 (14 ounce) can sweet condensed milk
1 cup chopped walnuts
1 teaspoon vanilla
⅛ teaspoon salt

In 2 quart saucepan, combine chocolate and milk over low heat. Cook until mixture has melted. Stir often. Remove from heat. Add walnuts, vanilla, and salt. Mix well. Spread mixture in 8 inch square baking pan. ◆Makes 60 pieces.

MOM'S CHOCOLATE FUDGE

3 cups sugar
1½ cups milk
7 level teaspoons cocoa
2 teaspoons butter
½ teaspoon butter
1 teaspoon vanilla

In medium saucepan, combine sugar, milk, and cocoa. Cook over medium heat. Stirring little until mixture makes a soft ball stage. Drop a small amount of mixture in a cup of cold water to check. After fudge reaches soft ball stage, remove from heat. Add butter and vanilla. Beat until slightly firm. Pour mixture on butter coated plate. Cut into squares.

THREE MINUTE FUDGE

■*(Microwave)*

3½ cups confectioners sugar

½ cup cocoa

½ cup margarine

¼ cup milk

1 teaspoon vanilla

½ cup chopped dry roasted nuts

In 2 quart microwave safe bowl, combine sugar and cocoa. Place margarine on top of mixture. Pour milk over mixture. Do not stir. Microwave on high 3 minutes. Mix well. Add vanilla and nuts. Coat 8x8 inch pan with cooking spray. Pour mixture into pan. Cool. Cut into squares.

CHOCOLATE CRAVING CLUSTERS

2 cups peanut butter

1 (16 ounce) package semisweet chocolate chips

1 (12 ounce) salted peanuts

In large saucepan, combine peanut butter and chips. Heat over low heat until mixture has melted. Add peanuts. Mix well. Drop mixture by teaspoonful on waxed paper. Cool. ◆Makes 4 dozen.

Colorado has the highest average altitude of any state in the nation, 6800 feet. Its lowest point of elevation is 3,350 feet above sea level at the bed of the lower Arkansas River, and its highest point is 14,431 feet at the peak of Mt. Elbert.

In **Estes Park, Colorado,** the Satirical World Art Museum houses 150 works by Jose Peres. His caustic portrayals of American political figures gave him the title of the "Will Rogers" of American Art.

DELIGHTFUL CLUSTERS

■*(Microwave)*

1⅔ cups peanut butter chips
2 tablespoons shortening
1½ cups crushed thin pretzel sticks
1 cup honey graham cereal
½ cup sliced almonds

In medium microwave safe bowl, combine peanut butter chips and shortening. Microwave at high 1½ minutes. Stir. Microwave until mixture is melted and smooth. Add pretzels, cereal, and almonds. Drop mixture by heaping tablespoons on waxed paper. Cool. ◆Makes 15 clusters.

MUDFLAP CHOCOLATE DROPS

2 cups milk chocolate chips
1 teaspoon shortening
½ cup raisins
½ cup walnuts

In medium saucepan, combine chocolate chips and shortening. Heat on low heat until melted. Add raisins and walnuts. Mix well. Drop mixture by tablespoonfuls onto waxed paper. Chill. ◆Makes 2 dozen.

LITTLE DIFFERENT PEANUT BRITTLE

1⅓ cups peanut butter chips
1½ cups butter, melted
1¾ cups sugar
3 tablespoons light corn syrup
3 tablespoons water

Butter 15½x10½x1 inch jelly roll pan. Sprinkle peanut butter chips evenly onto bottom of pan. In 2 quart saucepan, combine butter, sugar, corn syrup, and water. Cook over medium heat 35 minutes. Remove from heat and spread mixture over peanut butter chips. Cool. Break into pieces. ◆Makes 1¾ pounds.

CANDIED PRETZEL TREATS

■ *(Microwave)*

1 (16 ounce) bar almond bark
2 tablespoons oil
2 dozen pretzels
½ cup confectioners sugar

In 2 quart casserole, microwave almond bark and oil at medium high heat 3 to 4 minutes or until melted. Dip pretzel in mixture. Roll in sugar. Place on waxed paper and chill. ◆Makes 24 pretzels.

You can take a ride on the restored 1877 Georgetown Loop Railroad between **Georgetown** and **Silver Plume, Colorado.** To cover the two miles the railroad spirals 4.5 miles and rises 600 feet. It is so steep that a trestle actually doubles back over the tracks at Devil's Gate High Bridge.

The original turn-of-the-century company mining town of **Cokedale, Colorado,** is still intact. When the coal mines closed in 1947, the American Smelting and Refining Company sold homes in the town to its employees for $100 a room and $50 a lot.

SMOOTH CHOCOLATE SAUCE
(Diabetic)

2½ tablespoons granulated brown sugar substitute
2 tablespoons unsweetened cocoa
2 teaspoons cornstarch
1 cup skim milk
¼ teaspoon vanilla

In small saucepan, combine brown sugar, cocoa, cornstarch, and milk, over medium heat. Cook mixture until it begins to boil, cook 1 minute, stirring constantly. Remove from heat. Add vanilla. ◆Makes ¾ cup.

Per serving (1 tablespoon): *Exchanges– Free; Calories–14; Carbohydrates– 2 gm*

CHOCOLATE GLAZE
■*(Microwave)*

1 tablespoon cocoa
1 tablespoon margarine or butter
1 tablespoon water
½ cup confectioners sugar

In small bowl, combine all ingredients. Mix well. Microwave on high 20 to 30 seconds.

FLUFFY CREAM FROSTING

(Low fat/Low cal)

2 cups whipping cream
¼ cup confectioners sugar
1 teaspoon vanilla

In small bowl, combine all ingredients. With electric mixer, at medium speed until stiff peaks form. ◆Makes 4 cups.

Per serving (1 tablespoon): *Calories–28; Protein–0 gm; Fat– 3 gm; Carbohydrates–1 gm; Cholesterol–10 mm; Sodium– 3 mg*

DELICIOUS BUTTER FROSTING

½ cup butter or margarine
1 (16 ounce) package confectioners sugar
4 to 6 tablespoons milk
1½ teaspoons vanilla

In large bowl, combine butter 3 tablespoons of milk and vanilla, add confectioners sugar and beat with electric mixer on low speed until smooth. Add rest of milk. On medium speed, beat until light and fluffy, about 1 minute. ◆Makes 2½ cups.

EASY PIE CRUST

1 cup flour
3 tablespoons sugar
½ cup margarine, softened

In large bowl, combine all ingredients. Mix well. Press dough into 8 or 9 inch pie pan. ◆Makes 1 pie crust.

Don't break the red marble in the **Colorado State Capitol Building,** it can't be replaced. All of the only known deposit of "Beulah Red" marble in the world went into the Colorado State Capital, with the exception of a few small pieces around the fireplace in the Pueblo Courthouse. It was found in the Greenhorn Mountain foothills and installed between 1894 and 1900.

GRAHAM CRACKER CRUST

1½ cups crushed graham crackers
⅓ cup sugar
½ cup butter or margarine, melted

Preheat oven to 350 degrees. In medium bowl, combine all ingredients. Mix well. Press mixture firmly into bottom and sides of 9 inch pie pan. Bake 10 minutes. ◆Makes 1 crust.

Tips & Tidbits

Grilling
Camping and RVing
Phone Numbers
Travel Journal

Eldorado Canyon south of **Boulder, Colorado,** is one of the birthplaces of rock climbing in the U.S. There are hundreds of established routes for climbers of all abilities. Ivy Baldwin, daredevil tightrope walker, made 86 trips across Eldorado Canyon on a tightrope 585 feet above the ground. His last was a successful one in 1948 at the age of 82.

TOP TIPS IN GRILLING

• Let beef stand a few minutes after grilling. You will have a tastier piece of meat.

• When handling steaks, use tongs or a spatula instead of a fork, so you won't pierce the meat during cooking and allow the juices to seep out.

• Zippered plastic food storage bags are great for mess free marinating.

• The sooner the grill is cleaned after using, the easier cleaning will be.

• To prevent food from sticking to the grill, spray the cold grill with cooking spray or brush with vegetable oil.

• Avoid over mixing ground beef before grilling.

• If using bamboo skewers, soak them in water for about an hour before grilling to prevent them from burning.

• Soaking corn in cold water helps tenderize it and helps prevent the husks from burning while grilling.

• If you don't have a grill basket, a sheet of heavy duty foil that has a few holes poked in it also works.

• Salt meats after grilling.

• Trim excess fat from meat before grilling.

- Tougher cuts of meat should be tenderized by marinating or pounding with a meat mallet.

- Do not return cooked meat to a plate that was in contact with raw meat.

- Barbecue sauce is best applied towards the end of cooking to prevent burning.

GRILLING IT RIGHT

Heating the Grill

Gas grills heat 5 to 10 minutes before cooking.

Charcoal grills, light coals approximately 30 to 45 minutes before putting meat on the grill.

Temperature of Coals

The temperature of the coals is important for successful grilling. If the coals are too hot, the outside of the food can become charred and overcooked before the inside is properly cooked.

Controlling Flare-ups

Flare-ups are caused by fat and meat juices dripping onto hot coals and causing sudden small blazes.
1. Raise grill rack.
2. Remove a few coals.
3. Spread the coals further apart.
4. Cover grill.
5. Remove food from grill.
6. Mist fire with water.

The Manitou and Pikes Peak Cog Railway, the country's highest railroad, goes from Colorado Springs to the top of Pikes Peak. It makes a vertical gain of 7,539 feet (846 feet per mile) in its 46,158 feet climb. This is longer than any of the famous cogwheel rails in Switzerland. Along the route are bristlecone pines, estimated to be about 2,000 years old, among the oldest living things on earth.

The entire town of **Ouray, Colorado,** is a National Historic District. The quaint Victorian town has no traffic lights, fast food, malls or freeways–just charm and beau- tiful mountain scenery. Parts of the movies "True Grit" and "How the West Was Won" were filmed here. U.S. Highway 550 between Ouray and Silverton is called the Million Dollar Highway because the roadbed contains low grade gold ore.

Equipment and Accessories to Have on Hand

1. A stiff wire brush or scraper for brushing and scraping away burnt on food from the bars or griddle.
2. Gas lighter for barbecues without an automatic lighter.
3. Long handled tongs for turning and moving food from the grill.
4. Meat turner for lifting hamburgers, fish, etc.
5. Long sharp knife for carving large pieces of meat.
6. Heatproof gloves.
7. Water spray bottle to subdue flare–ups.

Approximate Cooking Time

Most beef cuts are best grilled over medium heat.

Medium Rare to Medium

Ribeye steak
¾ inch — 6 to 8 minutes
1 inch — 11 to 14 minutes

Porterhouse/ T-Bone Steak
¾ inch — 10 to 12 minutes
1 inch — 14 to 16 minutes

Top Loin Steak
¾ inch — 10 to 12 minutes
1 inch — 15 to 18 minutes

Tenderloin Steak
1 inch — 13 to 15 minutes

Top Sirloin Steak
¾ inch to 1 inch — 13 to 16 minutes
Boneless 1 inch — 17 to 21 minutes

Flank Steak
1½ to 2 lb. — 17 to 20 minutes

Top Round Steak
¾ inch — 8 to 9 minutes

Ground Beef patties
¼ lb. — 11 to 13 minutes
½ lb. — 13 to 15 minutes

Grilling Time for Vegetables

5-10 minutes

Carrot pieces or small whole Carrots

Whole Mushrooms

New Potatoes or Potato pieces

Small Whole Onions or ½ inch slices

Whole Asparagus Spears

10-15 Minutes

Bell Pepper strips 1 inch

Eggplant slices ¼ inch

Zucchini or Yellow Squash slices
    ¾ inch

Whole Green Beans

20-30 Minutes

Corn on the Cob

Artifacts of the Clovis people, generally believed to be the first wide-spread group of humans in the New World, are displayed at the Blackwater Draw Museum near **Clovis, New Mexico.** The evidence of America's earliest inhabitants was discovered in 1932. Displayed are the unique, fluted spear points used to hunt wooly mammoths about 11,000 years ago.

The Cathedral of Saint Francis of Assisi in **Santa Fe, New Mexico,** has the oldest representation of the Madonna in the United States. The wooden statue has been on display in the church for more than 300 years.

RVers AND VEHICLES ON THE MOVE

Gas Saving Tips

1. Observe the speed limit. Fuel economy typically decreases at speeds above 55 mph.

2. Use cruise control when it is safe to do so. Maintaining a constant speed will, in most cases, reduce fuel consumption.

3. Be conservative with the gas pedal. Do not apply any more throttle than necessary to get moving.

4. Make sure that your tires are properly inflated and your wheels in correct alignment.

5. Check and replace the air filter regularly. A dirty filter can cause up to 10 percent increase in fuel consumption.

6. Maintain your vehicle on a regular basis. Regular tune-ups and oil changes will keep your RV or vehicle operating smoothly.

7. Avoid carrying extra weight. An extra 100 pounds will reduce a typical car's fuel economy one to two percent. Motorhome results may vary, but any increase in fuel economy is a welcome one.

8. Using your air conditioner while driving instead of rolling down your windows will actually save money.

ASLEEP AT THE WHEEL

Road Etiquette

- Road rage is dangerous. Keep a cool head
- Dim your headlights for any approaching vehicle, even if he does not dim his.
- Keep in the right lane except when passing another vehicle.
- Always signal your intention to turn or change lanes well in advance.
- Keep you headlights on in the day time as a safety factor.
- Do not throw anything out of a vehicle window.
- Do not hog the highway.
- Do not empty your holding tanks while driving down the road.
- Be friendly. Wave to oncoming RV as you meet.

Sometimes you just can't get away. In 1848 a treaty after war with Mexico gave the U.S. the village of **Las Cruces, New Mexico.** About 60 families who preferred the Mexican government moved across the Rio Grande and created the town of Mesilla in 1850. But in 1854 Mexico sold the U.S. a 300,000 square mile strip of land, and Mesilla became part of the United States.

In **New Mexico** Taos Pueblo's multitiered adobe dwelling is one of the oldest continuously inhabited communities in the U.S. About fifty families live there. They get their water from the river and bake bread in outdoor ovens as their ancestors have done for the past 1,000 years. The remainder of the Taos-Tiawa families (4,000) live on the reservation in homes with modern conveniences.

DON'T TRIP ON ME

Camping Etiquette

- No claim jumping.
- Mind your fellow camper's personal space.
- Don't let your pets roam free.
- Avoid loud engine revving.
- Don't play your radio or TV too loud.
- Never dump waste water from holding tanks on campgrounds.
- Don't leave porch or entry lights on all night.
- Do not cut trees for firewood.
- Keep peace and quiet.
- Don't leave your campsite unclean.
- Always put out your campfire before leaving.

DID YOU KNOW?

- If you get a splinter, try scotch tape. Just place over the splinter, then pull tape off.
- Use meat tenderizer for a bee sting. It does the trick.
- Can't get coffee filters apart? Turn the stack inside out.
- If your cabinet doors or drawers keep getting stuck, try rubbing the edges with an unlit candle.
- Remove stale odors in the wash by adding baking soda.

- Tin coffee cans make excellent containers for cookies.

- Can't sleep? Try this. Mix 2 tablespoons honey and two tablespoons apple cider vinegar. For insomnia take one tablespoon at bedtime. For colds take twice a day.

- Place two lawn and leaf bags under your sleeping bag to help keep it clean.

- Sprinkling red pepper in areas where you are having trouble with ants will help keep them away.

- Use a tree limb to hold your paper towels.

- Coat the underside of the pan with liquid soap before placing it on an open fire. It will make clean up easier.

- To remove plastered bugs from the front of your motorhome or vehicle do the following. Mix one cap baking soda with enough water to create a creamy paste. Use a soft brush and apply to wet surface. Anything organic just dissolves away. Rewax the surface after cleaning.

- Never leave food in a tent. Food may invite unwanted friends who may tear up your tent.

- Cleanliness at a campsite is a must. Clutter, garbage, food, and dirty dishes attracted animals and insects.

- Lock your car or RV at night.

- Keep valuables in your trunk.

Eighty cowboys tried to kill Lawman Elfigo Baca after he arrested one of their friends in **Reserve, New Mexico.** The shack in which he took shelter had a floor 18 inches above the ground and gave him a place to hide. During a 33 hour gun battle in 1884, over 4,000 shots were fired into the building, but Baca emerged unhurt.

The Palace of the Governors in **Santa Fe, New Mexico,** is the oldest continuously used public building in the U.S. It was a seat of government under Spanish, American Indian, Mexican and U.S. Territorial rule, and has been a museum of New Mexican history and culture since 1911. Native artisans sell their wares from the porch.

WHERE'S THE INSECT REPELLENT?

Camping List
(Check it twice)

1. Tent
2. Sleeping bags
3. Cooking and eating utensils
4. Food
5. Flashlight
6. Spare batteries
7. Stove with fuel or grill
8. Matches
9. Lantern
10. Insect repellent
11. First aid kit
12. Binoculars
13. Sunglasses
14. Compass
15. Maps
16. Rope
17. Knife
18. Rain gear
19. Small tool kit
20. Sewing kit
21. Candles
22. Soap and towels
23. Boots
24. Paper towels
25. Toilet paper
26. Small battery radio
27. Aluminum foil

WHAT'S THAT SMELL?

Getting Prepared
Personal Items List

1. Toothbrush and tooth paste
2. Hairbrush and comb
3. Shampoo and conditioner
4. Manicure set
5. Deodorant
6. Suntan lotion
7. Skin moisturizer
8. Tissues
9. Toilet tissue
10. Soap
11. Towels
12. Sewing kit
13. Plastic bags
14. Medicines
15. Personal hygiene items
16. Shower shoes
17. Shaving supplies
18. Cosmetics

Who built the miraculous corkscrew stairs leading to the choir loft in Loretto Chapel in **Santa Fe, New Mexico**? A carpenter appeared mysteriously, built the staircase without nails or visible support beams-using only a T-square, hammer, saw and tub of water for bending wood. He then left without leaving his name or taking any money.

At **Albuquerque, New Mexico,** the world's longest aerial tramway carries you from the desert floor, above canyons and lush forests 2.7 miles to the top of 10,387 feet Sandia Peak. There you are treated to a panoramic view of 11,000 square miles.

SPECIAL HELP LINES

Emergency Assistance (Police, Fire, Ambulance)	911
Missing Children	1-800 843-5678
Child Search	1-800 833-3773
Poison Control	1-800 222-1222
Environmental Protection	1-800 438-2474
Family Doctor	_____
Family Dentist:	_____
Bank:	_____

HELP!
MY CREDIT CARDS ARE LOST!

American Express	1-800 528-2122
Dinners Club	1-800 234-6377
Discover	1-800 347-7309
Mastercard	1-800 307-7309
Visa	1-800 336-3386

IF THE BED GETS WET

Hotels and Motels

Best Western	1-800-528-1234
Comfort Inns	1-800-228-5150
Courtyard by Marriott	1-800-321-2211
Days Inn	1-800-325-2525
Econo Lodge	1-800-553-2666
Embassy Suites	1-800-362-2779
Fairfield Inns	1-800-228-2800
Friendship Inns	1-800-453-4511
Hampton Inns	1-800-426-7866
Hilton Hotels	1-800-445-8667
Holiday Inns	1-800-465-4329
Howard Johnson	1-800-654-2000
Hyatt Hotels	1-800-233-1234
La Quinta Inns	1-800-531-5900

Marriott Hotels	1-800-228-9290
Motel 6	1-800-466-8356
Quality Inns	1-800-228-5151
Ramada Inns	1-800-228-2828
Red Lion Inns	1-800-547-8010
Red Roof Inns	1-800-843-7663
Rodeway Inns	1-800-228-2000
Super 8 Motels	1-800-800-8000
Travel Lodge	1-800-578-7878

JUST IN CASE

Automobile Rentals

Ace Rent-A-Car	1-800-243-3443
Alamo	1-800-327-9633
Avis	1-800-831-2847
Budget	1-800-527-0700
Dollar Rent-A-Car	1-800-800-9853
Enterprise	1-800-325-8007
Hertz Rent-A-Car	1-800-654-3131
National Car Rental	1-800-227-7368
Payless Car Rental	1-800-729-5377
Rent-A-Wreck	1-800-421-7253
Thrifty Car Rental	1-800-367-2277

Airlines

Alaska Airlines	1-800-426-0333
American West	1-800-235-2929
American Airlines	1-800-433-7300
Continental	1-800-525-0280
Delta Airlines	1-800-221-1212
Southwest Airlines	1-800-435-9792
United Airlines	1-800-241-6522
U.S. Air	1-800-428-4322

Bus Lines

Greyhound	1-800-231-2222
Trailways	1-800-343-9999

The Big Rock Candy Mountain is located on Highway 89 south of **Richfield, Utah.** It looks like a mound of caramel. The hit folk song was written by Harry McClintock and sung by Burl Ives, but neither of them ever saw the mountain. Folk experts say the original song, with its "lemonade springs" and "lakes of stew" was sung by old-time hobos to lure young boys into a life on the road.

STAYING OUT OF HOT WATER

Ordering Special Gifts on the Road

Florists

Flower World	1-800 257-7880
1-800-Flowers	1-800 356- 9377

Gifts and Gift Baskets

Dial A Gift Basket	1-800 562-5950
Gift Basket Emporium	1-800 888-4490
Godiva Chocolatier	1-800 946-3482
Marrow's Nut House	1-800 374-6887
See's Candies	1-800 671-7337

IMPORTANT PHONE NUMBERS

TRAVEL JOURNAL

Special Travel Memories

_____

_____

_____

_____

_____

_____

_____

_____

_____

_____

_____

_____

_____

_____

_____

_____

_____

_____

_____

_____

_____

_____

_____

_____

_____

_____

Southern **Utah** has the country's largest grouping of national parks. Red sandstone arches, pillars, spires, canyons and cliffs offer some of the most spectacular scenery in the U.S. The five National Parks are: Arches, Bryce Canyon, Canyonlands, Capitol Reef and Zion.

The North Rim of the Grand Canyon is 1,000 feet higher than the more visited South Rim. It is a different climate zone and is heavily forested with blue spruce and alpine vegetation-in contrast with the arid South Rim. The North Rim is open May to October and receives only about ten percent of the visitors to the Grand Canyon.

Arizonans claim that "God created the Grand Canyon, but he lives in Sedona." Red rock scenery, cliff dwellings, petroglyphs and pictographs are abundant. Great art galleries are numerous. For those so inclined, the Sedona area is supposed to be a center of psychic energy. The area has over 3 million visitors a year, surpassed only by the Grand Canyon.

Craters of the Moon National Monument, 20 miles from **Arco, Idaho,** is 83 square miles that look like a sooty, black wasteland, but is a surreal cornucopia of lava cones, tubes, buttes, caves, craters and splatter cones. There has been no eruption of a volcano – instead lava flows from wounds in the earth's crust about every 2,000 years. The next flow is due at any time.

A small roadside park near **Grand Coulee, Washington,** has 175 windmills and whirligigs. The Gehrke Windmill Gardens' attractions are crafted from junk such as bedpans, bicycle wheels, broiler pans, hard hats and tractor seats. They are surrounded by flowers in gaily painted washing machine tubs.

The highest bungee jump in the Western Hemisphere is at **Fairview, Oregon.** Jumpers strapped into a full body harness with three to five bungee cords can dive off a 180 foot bridge.

The first rural paved road in the Pacific Northwest was the Historic Columbia River Highway. It runs along the foot of sheer cliffs of the Columbia River Gorge with spectacular views. It was built in 1916 by a concrete tycoon in an effort to get the **Oregon** legislature to let him build a highway up the length of the Columbia River.

The flamboyant and outrageous desert rat and one-time performer with Buffalo Bill's Wild West Show, Death Valley Scottie, supposedly had a secret gold mine. Although his friend, Chicago millionaire Albert Johnson, built the unique $2 million mansion, now know as Scottie's Castle in **Death Valley, Nevada** he never disputed Scottie's claim that gold from his mine had paid for it.

One of the most beautiful drives in America may be the 72 miles around Lake Tahoe in **California** and **Nevada**, with pines, craggy cliffs, aquamarine waters and the snow capped Sierra Nevada range. The second deepest lake in the United States was formed when faults created a canyon that was filled by a melting glacier.

The Star Wars film, "Return of the Jedi," used the groves of giant trees in the **Redwood National Park** on Highway U.S. 101 in Northern **California** as a location. The characters cruised through the forest on airborne cycles. The Tall Trees Grove has the world's tallest tree, the Libby Tree, which is 368 feet high and whose trunk measures over 14 feet across.

Just Around the Curve

The world's tallest thermometer rises above the Bun Boy Restaurant in the Mojave Desert town of **Baker, California.** It shows one foot for each degree of temperature up to the hottest recorded in the history of the Mojave, 134 degrees on July 10, 1913. The current temperature is recorded day and night and can be seen from I-15.

In the 1970's a group of dare-devil cyclists from **Marin County, California,** invented the all-terrain mountain bike (which accounts for half of all bikes on and off the roads) so they could cruise down the fire roads of Mount Tamalpais at the highest speed possible. On Highway 1, the signature peak of the San Francisco Bay area rises to an elevation of 2,586 feet.

Inspectors at 16 **California** agricultural inspection stations will ask you what fruits, vegetables or nuts you have in your vehicle and where you bought them. This is to control pests such as fruit flies and fungi that may be harmful to crops in California's gigantic agricultural industry. You may have to either eat certain foods or destroy them before entering the state.

Sara L. Winchester, heiress to the Winchester Rifle fortune, began building her Victorian mansion in **California** in 1884, and kept building until her death 34 years later. A team of carpenters and craftsmen worked constantly. Supposedly she thought that if the home was completed, she would die. It has 160 rooms, 3 elevators, 47 fireplaces, a stairway leading up to the ceiling and doors that open to blank walls.

Alaska (whose name means "great land of the west") contains America's northernmost, westernmost, and (because the Aleutian Islands stretch across the 180th meridian) the easternmost point. More than twice the size of Texas, if superimposed on the lower 48 states, it would stretch from the Atlantic to the Pacific.

The state of **Hawaii** is comprised of eight major islands, Niihau, Kauai, Oahu, Molokai, Maui, Lanai, Kahoolawe, and Hawaii (The Big Island). Measuring from its submarine base (3,280 fathoms) in the Hawaiian Trough to the top of the mountain (13,796 feet), Mauna Kea is the tallest mountain in the world with a combined height of 33,476 feet.

At **Pearl Harbor, Hawaii,** a simple white memorial marks the resting place for more than 1,100 members of the USS Arizona, sunk in the surprise Japanese bombing on December 7, 1941. More than 1.5 million people visit it annually, many of them Japanese. The USS Missouri, used for the 1945 ceremony in Tokyo Harbor that ended World War II, is moored alongside and is open for guided visits.

Index

Beef

A Robust Beef Brisket, 73

America's Favorite Roast, 69

Barbecue Spareribs, 71

*Burger Bites, 33

Colorado Beef Bake, 122

Connecticut Swiss Steak, 73

Corned Beef Ruebens, 75

Crock Pot Chuck Roast, 70

Fork Tender Short Ribs, 71

Get the Chill Out Beef Soup, 42

Grilled Onion Burgers, 68

*Just Ahead Potatoes and Beef, 121

Mad Max Beef Burgers, 67

Mexi Meat Loaf, 74

Mix and Forget It Roast, 70

Mix It Quick Meat Loaf, 74

Nebraska Beef and Mac Skillet, 114

Nevada Potatoes and Beef Bake, 122

No Fuss Veggie Beef Soup, 44

North Dakota Grilled Burgers, 68

Oklahoma Chicken Fried Steak, 76

Old Reliable Beef Pizza, 112

Out All Day Beef Stroganoff, 114

*Party Meatballs, 33

Quick Beef Topper, 75

Rest Stop Beef Barley Soup, 44

Route 66 Pot Roast, 70

Showing Off Cheeseburgers, 67

*Skillet Stew, 124

South Carolina Hearty Stew, 123

Speed Trap Burgers, 69

Texas Beef Stew, 123

Texas T-Bone, 72

Veggie Beef Soup, 43

Wyoming Oh So Delicious Beef, 72

Beverages

A Coffee Pickerupper, 11

After a Hike Cocktail, 11

*Cranberry Cool Down Coolers, 30

*Creamy Orange Frost, 30

Hot Juice Warm-Ups, 11

Making Condensed Milk, 14

Shake Awake Smoothie, 12

*Smooth Chocolate Sipper, 29

*Sunny Afternoon Slush, 29

Tailgate Party Punch, 13

Biscuits

Biscuit on a Stick, 148

Cheesey Top Biscuits, 150

Drop by Spoon Biscuits, 149

Good Morning Biscuits, 148

Never Fail to Please Biscuits, 149

Raisin Tasting Biscuits, 151

Yummy Cinnamon Biscuit, 150

Bread and Rolls

*Blueberry Nut Muffins, 143

Bumper to Bumper Cinnamon Rolls, 141

Bumpy Cheese Bread, 144

Butter Topped Bread, 145

Chocolate Chip Banana Bread, 143

Fast Fix'n Rolls, 147

Freedom Toast, 156

From Home Lemon Muffins, 142

*Fruit Muffins, 142

Hot Cheddar Bread, 144

Hot Off the Fire Bread, 146

Kentucky Spoonbread, 147

Massachusetts Brown Bread, 146

Nuts and Bolts Sticky Buns, 140

Oklahoma Indian Fry Bread, 145

Old Timers Hardtack, 154

Quick Fix Doughnuts, 141

*Sunny Popovers, 151

C

*Cabbage and Apples Sweet Dish, 106

Cajun Beans and Sausage Over Rice, 136

California Chicken Salad, 58

California Cream Style Cornbread, 152

California Frosty Grapes, 23

Candied Pretzel Treats, 189

*Caramel Tasting Custard, 183

Casual Get Together Apple Salad, 53

Celery Around Pork Chops, 79

Cheese Tuna Balls, 21

Cheesey Top Biscuits, 150

Cheesy Chicken Tenders, 90

Chicken Pot Pie, 120

Chili Chicken or Pork Rub, 101

Chili and Tamale Casserole, 118

Chocolate Chip Banana Bread, 143

Chocolate Chip Ice Cream, 185

Chocolate Craving Clusters, 187

Chocolate Escape Pie, 165

Club House Cheese Spread, 27

Coast to Coast Pineapple Cake, 166

*Cock of the Walk Drumsticks, 90

Cold Day Chicken Noodle Soup, 42

Colorado Beef Bake, 122

Connecticut Swiss Steak, 73

Cook Don't Bake Brownies, 174

Crock Pot Chuck Roast, 70

Corned Beef Ruebens, 75

Country Fried Cornbread, 152

*Cranberry Cool Down Coolers, 30

Cranberry Freeze Salad, 52

Creamy Broccoli Soup, 37

Creamy Dip for Veggies, 17

Creamy Garlic Chicken, 88

*Creamy Orange Dip, 3

Creamy Orange Frost, 30

*Crispy Treats Bars, 176

Crock Pot Broccoli Cheese Soup, 38

Crock Pot Candied Carrots, 106

Crock Pot Caramel Apples, 182

Cruise America Pumpkin Pie, 162

Crusty Fried Catfish, 93

Cut to the Chase Pea Salad, 55

Cakes and Frostings

A Winner Cherry Coffeecake, 139

Angel in My Kitchen Cake, 168

Chocolate Glaze, 190

Coast To Coast Pineapple Cake, 166

Delicious Butter Frosting, 191

*Fluffy Cream Frosting, 191

Ice Cream Sandwich Cake, 169

Miracle Whip Chocolate Cake, 167

Pennsylvania Cheese Cake, 168

So Easy Chocolate Cake, 167

Special Blueberry Coffee Cake, 140

Upside Down Chocolate Cake, 166

Candy

Chocolate Craving Clusters, 187

Delightful Clusters, 188

Gimme a Brake Fudge, 186

Little Different Peanut Brittle, 189

Mom's Chocolate Fudge, 186

Mudflap Chocolate Drops, 188

Sweet Treat Fudge, 185

Three Minute Fudge, 187

Index

OTHER COOKBOOKS AVAILABLE FROM CREATIVE INDEAS PUBLISHING

To order, fill out enclosed order form.

BUSY WOMAN'S COOKBOOK A national bestseller by Sharon and Gene McFall. Over 350,000 copies sold. It has over 500 mouth-watering 3 and 4 ingredient recipes and more than 200 short stories and facts about famous and influential women. $16.95

COOKIN' WITH WILL ROGERS by Sharon and Gene McFall. Has over 560 delicious country cookin' recipes with over 100 Will Rogers quotes, 60 pictures and 50 stories of one of America's most beloved humorists. "Only a fool argues with a skunk, a mule or a cook." Will Rogers. $19.95.

HOME MADE BLESSINGS by Diane Reasoner. Over 400 excellent tasting recipes, straight forward instructions and ingredients that are found in any pantry. Inspirational sayings on every page that will brighten your day. $19.95.

MILD TO WILD MEXICAN COOKBOOK by Linda Burgett. Over 400 tantalizing recipes from south of the border. Every recipe tells you if it is hot, medium or mild-so you have no big surprises. Also has fun facts on ingredients. One word for this book—Wonderful. $16.95.

GET ME OUT OF THE KITCHEN by Sharon and Gene McFall. 500 easy to prepare recipes. Special low-fat and low-cal recipes as well as helpful cooking hints. A wonderful cookbook. $16.95.

COMING SOON

MY KIND OF COOKING: Everybody's Favorite 4 and 5 Ingredient Recipes by Shelley Plettl. Delicious crockpot, microwave, electric gril and other recipes to make life in the kitchen easier. $16.95.